MW01254258

The
CHINESE
SHAR-PEI

Ellen Weathers Debo

Title page: June Collins's Three Sisters' Ah Dah at one-and-a-half years of age. *Ah Dah* means "something special" in Chinese.

© 1986 by T.F.H. Publications, Inc. Distributed in the UNITED STATES by T.F.H. Publications, Inc., 211 West Sylvania Avenue, Neptune City, NJ 07753; in CANADA by H & L Pet Supplies Inc., 27 Kingston Crescent, Kitchener, Ontario N2B 2T6; Rolf C. Hagen Ltd., 3225 Sartelon Street, Montreal 382 Quebec; in CANADA to the Book Trade by Macmillan of Canada (A Division of Canada Publishing Corporation), 164 Commander Boulevard, Agincourt, Ontario M1S 3C7; in ENGLAND by T.F.H. Publications Limited, 4 Kier Park, Ascot, Berkshire SL5 7DS; in AUSTRALIA AND THE SOUTH PACIFIC by T.F.H. (Australia) Pty. Ltd., Box 149, Brookvale 2100 N.S.W., Australia; in NEW ZEALAND by Ross Haines & Son, Ltd., 18 Monmouth Street, Grey Lynn, Auckland 2 New Zealand; in SINGAPORE AND MALAYSIA by MPH Distributors (S) Pte., Ltd., 601 Sims Drive, #03/07/21, Singapore 1438; in the PHILIPPINES by Bio-Research, 5 Lippay Street, San Lorenzo Village, Makati Rizal; in SOUTH AFRICA by Multipet Pty. Ltd., 30 Turners Avenue, Durban 4001. Published by T.F.H. Publications, Inc. Manufactured in the United States of America by T.F.H. Publications, Inc.

Contents

Dedication

To all the dear, loving, four-legged
friends I have known, and in remembrance of
my Mum and Marty Gold,
two of my best human friends.

With Loving Appreciation

To my daughters, Kathy and Kris, for their help and secretarial skills, without which this book would read as one long sentence.

To my husband, Phil, for having the tolerance that's needed to live with an "animal nut."

Also, a very large "thank you" to all the people who took time to contribute, and a very special "thank you" to Matgo Law.

Matgo Law presents Miss Mimi Murphy and Eshaf's Hoi Toi Best of Opposite Sex at the First Annual Chinese Shar-pei Specialty Show.

Foreword

He has been called the Sharkskin Dog, the Chinese Bulldog, and the Chinese Fighting Dog, but he is far better known as the Chinese Shar-pei (or that funny little dog with all the wrinkles). Believed to have originated over 2,000 years ago and used primarily for fighting and for guarding homes and livestock, this breed suffered many setbacks along the way. Its numbers were few and far between when Mr. Matgo Law of Hong Kong, a knowledgeable and enthusiastic fancier dedicated to the preservation of this breed, pleaded for help in the April 1973 issue of *Dogs* magazine to save the Chinese Shar-pei from extinction. He was afraid that Hong Kong, now a British Crown Colony (but only until the end of this century), would again come under communist rule and that perhaps the few known Shar-peis would suffer the same fate as had befallen the earlier pets of mainland China.

An extract from the foreword of a book written by S. J. Tung, published by Dodd, Mead, and Company, entitled *One Small Dog*, informs us of the problems that pets of mainland China faced.

> Foreign visitors to China have reported that there are no dogs in that country. This is because all canines were killed in the mid-fifties when the Communists ordered

a nationwide campaign to annihilate the dogs of China. Not only dogs, but cats, sparrows, and rats were objects of government attention in an effort to save food for the people. The campaigns were drastic measures but seemed necessary in the face of famine.

Mr. Tung's story is that of a young boy who, in order to save his beloved dog, "Lucky," from the annihilate-the-dogs campaign that was carried out by the militia, smuggles him out of China and into British Hong Kong. His dog has a background similar to the fortunate Shar-peis who were saved by being imported to the United States.

We do know that when Matgo Law made his appeal in 1973, the breed was dying out. Not only had the number of Shar-peis been reduced by famine, but by high taxes, prejudice, and the sport of dog fighting as well. During the period of food shortages, anyone caught hiding a family pet was severely taxed; the dogs were then confiscated and put to death. Then there were the Chinese gamblers who, recognizing the unique protective quality of the Shar-pei coat and realizing the great potential these dogs had as pit fighters, crossbred Shar-peis with the champion combatants or with any other canines that they thought would add strength and stamina to their own line of fighting dogs. The production of "winning warriors" was of great importance to these sportsmen, even though it would take a combination of breeds to produce them. So besides all the other threats to the Shar-pei's survival, this mongrelization only made matters worse.

Matgo Law had taken on quite a difficult task, for not only did he have to save the breed from extinction, but he also had to begin the job of purifying it. Covering many miles in his quest to acquire those specimens that resembled the original Shar-pei, he gathered up all the dogs he could, following leads from friends and dealers, and, at least in one case, even secured one from the local dog cart. Armed, then, with a thorough knowledge of dogs and dog breeding, Mr. Law attempted to recreate and reestablish the Chinese Shar-pei as a pure breed, and this ultimately led to his plea for help.

Pictures and a description of the breed were included in the *Dogs* magazine article, and within a short time the American people rallied around Mr. Law to save this unusual-looking canine from oblivion. Since the Shar-pei was often a farmer's or poor man's dog, usually left to hunt for its own food and shelter, only the fittest and most intelligent survived. This was indeed fortunate for the breed today, since the limited number of these dogs necessitated close inbreeding (without the normal regard for quality and intelligence) in order to propagate them.

Response to Matgo Law's appeal was tremendous, and from the dozen or more dogs known to exist at that time, there are now over 6,000 individuals registered with the Chinese Shar-pei Club of America. With the addition of dogs and puppies as yet not registered, we speculate that there may be as many as 7,000 or more of these dogs in the United States at the present time. The Chinese Shar-pei is by no means a rare and endangered breed any more.

Chinese Shar-pei puppies present an appealing picture with wrinkles and rolls in abundance. As they mature, they grow into a large percentage of their coat, and it is not uncommon for a very wrinkled puppy to end up as a fairly tight-coated adult; however, loose skin should be maintained under the throat and at the back of the neck and over the shoulders. Although the most common colors are fawn, black, and cream, additional and exotic colors such as red, chocolate, blue, and silver are appearing with far more frequency. There is also a spotted variety known as the "flowered" dog.

While the Chinese Shar-pei does make, on the whole, an excellent family pet, care in handling and very gentle early training should be emphasized lest one forget that he is, after all, a descendant of China's fighting dogs. Ideally, the Shar-pei temperament is that of a loving protector of his family. He is wary of and slow to make friends with strangers, he is extremely intelligent, and he is very easily housebroken. For this reason, males make as good house pets as females, quickly learning the rights and wrongs of where they may or may not lift a leg.

Ultimately, a Shar-pei's tongue should be black; its tail should always be carried high, whether in a tight curl, a loose curl, or straight up and over the back. Ears should be small and tight, the muzzle should be hippopotamus-shaped, the body should be square and substantial, the coat should be short and harsh, and

Ah Fook **(top)**, a real fighter on the island of Macau. Note the narrow nose. Adam of Ma's Kennels **(bottom)** at three years, a dog from Hong Kong.

Ah Lou, owned by Mr. Ho Yu Hong, was eight years old when this photo was taken. Lou is a famous stud dog.

the animal's movement should be sound. He should look as formidable as he believes himself to be.

The average lifespan of the Chinese Shar-pei at present appears to be approximately eight to twelve years. With time to acclimatize themselves to countries outside their native China, with careful and conscientious breeding programs, and with new cures for some of their canine ailments, we hope their longevity may be extended by several more years.

There is nothing like owning and being owned by a Shar-pei. One doesn't open the door to let in a family pet; one opens the heart to take in a family member.

The late Marty Gold of House of Gold pictured with Down-Homes Cream Woo.

12

Chapter 1

History and Development

Scattered information gathered over the centuries leads us to believe that the Shar-pei originated as long ago as the Han Dynasty (206 BC–220 AD). The actual creation and development at that time is purely speculative, as much of the breed's early history has been lost since the communists gained control of China. Quite possibly, the birth of our breed took place in the small town of Dah Let in the province of Kwun Tung. The Shar-pei is believed to have either descended from or shared a common origin with the smooth-coated Chow Chow (because of the blue-black mouths and tongues), possibly the Great Pyrenees (a source of the double dewclaws), and the Tibetan Mastiff. The first Shar-pei may have appeared as a mutation

Translated, the name *Shar-pei* becomes "Sandy dog"— *Shar* meaning sand of a gritty texture and *pei* meaning dog. This presents us with a very definite description of the unique prickly texture and extreme short length of the coat, which resembles a piece of sandpaper. This rare coat was of such importance to the early developers of the breed that it became the instrument through which the Shar-pei was described and named. No other canine possesses this extraordinary type of hair. It is, indeed, a distinguishing characteristic.

Unfortunately for our Shar-peis, they were not bred as lap dogs to wallow in palatial luxury; they were considered common. The lucky ones were working companions to peasant farmers, protectors of home and property. Incidentally, in China *any* dog that protects property is called a fighting dog, whereas in America they are referred to as guard dogs. Some Shar-peis were used to hunt wild game, usually wild pigs, in China. It should be mentioned, however, that these dogs probably would not be good retrievers, for they have the terrier instinct of shaking that which they catch for the kill. The unlucky Shar-peis, probably the majority, were pit dogs bred to fight for their lives and "give their all" in order to fill their gambling owners' purses.

The dog was bred feature by feature, by trial and error and piece by piece, until the unique traits that make him so unusual were perfected for his own protection. The black tongue of the Chinese Shar-pei is a rare and important characteristic possibly inherited from the Chow Chow. These two breeds are the only ones, known at present, in which tongue color is so important. It was believed in ancient times that the dark mouth of the Chow Chow, exposed when the dog was barking, helped frighten away evil spirits. Although a spotted tongue (sometimes referred to as a "flowered" tongue) is more desirable than a pink tongue, the blue or black tongue, gums, and roof of the mouth are the ultimate achievement in a breeder's program. In fact, in one Hong Kong dog registry, The Kow Loon Kennel Club Association, the black tongue is so highly regarded that Shar-peis with pink or spotted tongues simply are not accepted

The extraordinary coat, the Shar-pei's suit of armor, may have started out as a mutation of a longer coat or from a crossbreeding of two different ancestors. Some enterprising Chinese saw the potential defense the coat offered its wearer and developed it further over many, many years until the bristled texture, the short length, and the layers of wrinkles that we find so appealing today were achieved.

The correct texture of the coat, as described by the Chinese, should be extremely harsh to the touch but at the same time deceive the eye by appearing soft like velour. The coat *does* have a velvety texture when one strokes the dog from head to tail, but if this same coat is stroked against the grain (from tail to head), it may become abrasive, producing a burning, itching sensation for some people. Nature equipped the Shar-pei with this irritant for a reason: to discourage other animals from grasping them with their mouths. And, of course, this desirable trait was sought after and perpetuated by breeders of fighting dogs.

We cannot deny that some Shar-pei owners suffer to some extent with their bristle-coated companions at one time or another. There are owners who are allergic to the Shar-pei coat, as evidenced by blisters and welts which may last several hours or days and then fade away, while others may possibly break out in a rash which disappears shortly. Those unfortunate souls who suffer from an allergic reaction to their pets can find relief by having their doctors prescribe a hypoallergenic preparation. Under normal conditions, the effect of brushing against the harsh coat is not very severe, but an animal under stress may create a problem for those owners who are sensitive to the prickly pelage.

As a defense mechanism, the Shar-pei has the ability to stiffen his already stiff coat, in the same way other dogs can raise the ruff around their necks and along their backs to exhibit aggressive behavior when, for example, danger threatens. Since the Shar-pei coat normally stands away from the body, it really can become very uncomfortable to the touch if the dog is aroused in some way.

Just as stiff coats are characteristic of the Shar-pei, so are ears and ear set. The ears should be small, and the smaller the better. It is reported that in some of the ancient Shar-peis, the ears were as small as a human thumbnail, just large enough to cover the opening. One explanation for the small size is that a tiny ear offers an attacker very little to get a hold of and makes it even more difficult to hold on to. From a distance, a Shar-pei's ears should not even be visible, blending tightly into the forehead. This type of ear does not occur as a result of manually cropping, taping, or bending them, but it can, and should be, achieved through selective breeding.

Though the ears are set tightly to the head, they still have a great deal of maneuverability and are independent of each other. While listening to different noises, a Shar-pei flicks its ears in and out to the side in much the same way a horse does. When he's upset, he pulls the ears back and out to the side; and when his feelings have been hurt, the ears are pulled down alongside his face. Ears are forward and head is lowered when he's on the alert or given a challenge. It should be mentioned that a Shar-pei's ears

At one time the Chinese Shar-pei was used to hunt wild boar and other animals, since its sensitive nose provided it with great tracking ability **(top).** Bedlam's Yo Ki Hi, owned by the author, has retained most of her wrinkling as an adult **(bottom).**

should never stand straight up; this is known in the dog fancy as "prick ears," as seen on German Shepherd Dogs.

The Shar-pei's tail should denote bravery. Three descriptions are mentioned, in order of preference, in the breed standard sent by Matgo Law. The first is the tightly-curled tail, described as a "coin" tail. The second tail set is the loose curl, and the third is carried in an arch over the back. The common denominator for all three is that they are carried high, exposing the anus. A Shar-pei with his tail carried out like a bird dog (an Irish Setter, for instance) or tucked between his legs, like the Borzoi, is not desirable, for it fails to suggest, in our breed, a picture of confidence. Occasionally puppies are born with three-quarter-length tails, half tails, and even no tails at all; however, these are faults to be bred out. With three tail carriages from which to choose, it should be easy to achieve one of these through careful breeding. A breeder should always strive for the ultimate goal set forth in the standard, which, in this case, is the coin tail.

The all-important folds of skin on a Shar-pei are just that: all important. The adult dog should retain wrinkling on the face to present a scowling and dignified countenance. When these dogs were first bred, the loose folds over the shoulders provided a defense in case they were attacked from behind; these folds enabled them to twist around and break the hold. The abundant, heavy dewlaps (folds of skin around the throat) provided protection for the throat. Too little in the way of loose skin offered small protection, and too many folds on the body were detrimental, as they could easily be torn or be a hindrance to maneuverability. So the right amount of wrinkles was, and still is, imperative in the breeding of Shar-peis.

Unfortunately, two common myths have had their impact on the fronts (the forepart of the body as viewed head on, i.e., forelegs, chest, brisket, and shoulder line). One belief by old-time dog-fighting fanciers was that toes turned out helped the dog with balance. Also, the Chinese crawling dragon with his feet pointed east and west was considered a sign of strength. As a result of this kind of thinking and poor breeding practices, many of the Shar-peis we see today have extremely bad fronts. Forelegs should be straight, with feet facing forward. Hindlegs should not be so straight, as those of the Chow Chow; a little more angulation is called for in the standard, as the early Shar-peis needed to be able to twist, turn, and leap with a great deal of agility. Four good, sound legs able to withstand impact were, and continue to be, important.

The body of the Shar-pei should be square: the chest, broad and deep; the neck, strong and full, set well on the shoulders. The lowest part of the backline should be similar to that of the Bull-dog, yet the topline should not be as sunken. The overall appearance should be that of a muscular, active, short-coupled dog (many specimens now tend to have too much leg for their length of body).

It is hard to describe the lovely eye type as designed by nature and not one accomplished by surgery. [*Editor's note:* Some Shar-peis are afflicted with entropion, an ocular defect in which the in-rolling eyelids bring lashes or skin hairs into direct contact with the cornea; this problem can be corrected through surgery.] Eyes are referred to in the standard as dark, small, and sunken (a lighter color eye being found in cream and light fawn dogs). This eye set was just another of the protection devices bred into these dogs (especially those that were going to be used for dog fighting), for large or protruding eyes would have been easily injured.

The Shar-pei mouth is described as having teeth strong and level, closing in a scissors bite, i.e., the top teeth close tightly over the bottom teeth. The canine teeth are somewhat curved (this I haven't found to be a general rule); supposedly, this was to cause difficulty in freeing the grip. Undershot mouths—the bottom teeth closing over the top teeth—are very undesirable in a Shar-pei but acceptable in a Bulldog. Overshot mouths, whereby the upper teeth leave a gap between them and the bottom teeth when closed, should be avoided.

Some Shar-pei breeders explain to novices that those individuals with long, soft coats are much nicer to hold and, therefore, are easier to live with. In fact, the Chinese Shar-pei Club of America breed standard calls for three types of coats: the short, bristly coat; the soft, short coat; and the long, soft coat. The desire to own a longhaired Shar-pei is understandable, but long coats did not figure in the original description that accompanied Matgo Law's plea to American dog fanciers. As we have already discussed, the name *Shar-pei* means sandy coat, sandy in the sense of

A solid bluish-black tongue is preferred, according to the CSPCA breed standard; however, spotted or "flowered" tongues, like the one on this dog **(top, left)**, are acceptable. When viewed from the front, a Shar-pei's forelegs should be straight **(top, right).** The feet may turn out slightly for balance. "Puff" **(bottom)** was one of two longhaired puppies in a litter of seven, the remaining littermates having had the characteristic short, harsh coats.

gritty and rough. A long, soft coat, while it may feel good to us, probably would not have helped save the Shar-pei from extinction, either in the dog fighting pits or in the wild where it had to forage and hunt wild beasts. Our wrinkled friends needed their short, harsh coats to survive; this is why Shar-pei breeders who purport to be purists feel strongly about preserving this peculiar and useful feature.

The intelligence of the Shar-pei is remarkable. They are natural guard dogs, fiercely defensive of their home, loved ones, and possessions. Puppies seem to learn this trait from their mothers, who give them lessons in self-defense from weaning time until they leave the nest. Some bitches have a stronger influence on their puppies than others in this respect. What follows is a story about Ausables China Blue, better known as "Snuffy," who revealed to me her strong maternal instincts while giving birth to her first litter of pups.

"My first Shar-pei litter born naturally was a traumatic affair. After it was all finished, I was reduced to a shaking, quivering mass of nerves. I had attended many whelpings of several dog breeds for over 25 years, but they hadn't equipped me psychologically for anything so remote as the experience I was about to have. Snuffy (Ausables China Blue) was ready. She was panting, upset, and anxious—not enough to stop eating—but that was typical. She'd been known to stop and eat while breeding, fighting, and playing. Food was Snuff's main concern in life, apart from her puppies.

"To start with, I was nervous. This was my first litter of those precious Shar-peis, those rare dogs that we had gone into debt to own. It was up to Snuff and me to pull us out of the red with a puppy or two to sell, and a puppy or two to keep (I didn't know then that Shar-peis can be addictive. The more you have, the more you want; parting with the pups would bring a terror to my heart even greater than that caused by a trip to the dentist's!)

"To get back to Snuff and me, here we were. All alone. Husband working nights, kids out, Snuff in her box. I, sitting on the floor, surrounded by all the paraphernalia that goes with whelping puppies. She was happy to have me there, and if ever I left the room, she cried and tried to follow. So, I stayed close, patting her head. Then the arrival of the first pup occurred. Lucky me. I got to help take the sac off her face (it was a girl), and Snuffy started to clean. That's when the transformation of Snuffy took place. As she licked her pup, she changed from Jekyll to Hyde. This precious pup was being rolled, tossed, and tumbled. She was not only being licked, but she was getting chewed and chomped on vigorously, and what appeared to me to be viciously. When the whole head disappeared into Snuffy's mouth and she chomped down, my stomach rolled and I felt faint. I tried retrieving the pup from this terrible monster, but I was suddenly facing a shark in the litter box. I never realized what large teeth she had, or that there were so many of them. Imagine my surprise when her contractions started again and her attention was diverted from the "remains" of the puppy. The pup was intact and yelling lustily and very forcibly, trying to seize a nipple.

"Well, that was the last pup of Snuff's I got to help with. She took over. While she was having the contractions, I was able to pet and comfort her. As soon as a pup arrived, I wasn't wanted. I wasn't even allowed to touch or even put my hand in the box. The three puppies that were to follow remained sexless until quite some time later.

"Somehow the nasty part of the Jekyll-Hyde character had also invaded my mind. By the time my husband arrived home, I had been through hell and back. I didn't stop him, even though I could have. When hearing the puppies cry, he made tracks for the back room and the monster that waited! I heard, "Snuffy, what a good girl! Let's see your babies!" This was immediately followed by a cry of surprise and pain. I must admit, he had courage of a sort; three times I heard him ask, and three times I heard the answer. Three then being the magic number, he emerged holding a damaged hand. He'd finally gotten the message.

"This is not how all Shar-pei dams behave during parturition, but occasionally you will run into one like this. Snuffy was a bitch that was descended from the old Chinese Fighting Dogs, a dam ready and willing to die in defense of her puppies. I have heard these bitches criticized because of their dispositions, but are they really to be condemned? They are just closer to nature. No puppies were ever better fed, more diligently tended, or carefully guarded than Snuffy's. If she'd had them in the wild, they would have survived, barring anything happening to Snuffy herself.

Ausables China Blue, known affectionately as "Snuffy." A true Shar-pei in every sense of the word and owned by the author.

Snuffy was a true Shar-pei. When the puppies were four weeks old, she was teaching them how to fight and defend themselves. Grabbing a leg and dragging the puppy about or grabbing his tail, she would gently torment that puppy until he couldn't take it any longer. He would fly into a frantic rage, and, grabbing whatever part of his mother he could, he would shake her skin and growl. That was Snuff's signal. He'd learned his lesson, and she would give him a lick or two, wag her tail, and go on to tease and torment the next. She would do this until she had elicited the same response from the whole litter. Snuffy was a very zealous guard dog (I never locked a door), she hated the veterinarian, and she didn't take to strangers. But apart from those times when she was fiercely defensive as a mother, she was loving, loyal, and intelligent—a Shar-pei that you had to respect."

22

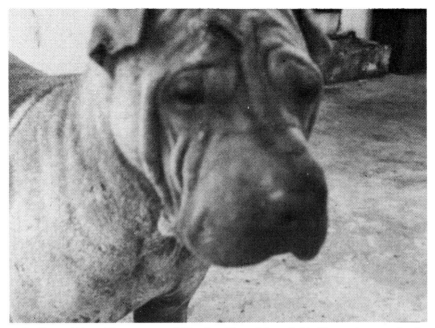

J. P. Chan of Hong Kong, owner of Cho Sun Kennel, breeds his Shar-peis according to the type called for in the original standard. Pictured is his Ahmac **(top)** at nine years. This male, ZL's "Y" Lee, belongs to Dick and Zell Llewellyn of Shoestring Acres, Alvin, Texas **(bottom).**

23

Hon. Ch. Go-Lo's Asia Mi-Na, by Down-Homes Prophet out of Down-Homes Fortune Cookie. Owner, Jo Ann and Duncan Redditt of Alexandria, Virginia.

24

Chapter 2

The Shar-pei Standard

The standard is the most important tool one has readily available to work with in breeding. It is the pattern for the ideal dog, specifying the desirable conformation, coloration, temperament, and characteristics that set a particular breed "type." It spells out in detail the differences, both apparent and subtle, that keep one breed separate from another; it publicizes a formula for the conformity of that breed; and it pigeonholes that group so it is easily recognized. Therefore, the German Shepherd Dog is bred to one standard and the Bulldog is bred to another, each dog presenting a totally different picture. Due to the uniqueness of each of these standards, the complete novice is able to easily distinguish one breed from another.

There is a challenge to the art of breeding dogs; only by constantly culling out and upgrading does one begin to follow the standard of perfection. In the United States there have been, unfortunately, three standards for the Chinese Shar-pei. If it is a hard task to conscientiously breed to one standard, imagine the difficulties created by the confusion of three. It spells disaster for the breed, and as each new standard becomes progressively looser, the Shar-pei becomes increasingly variable in type. Correct type and consistent characteristics are desired in all breeds, the standard being the goal toward which all dedicated fanciers strive.

The standard sent to America in 1973 by Matgo Law was the combined knowledge of many owners and breeders in the Orient.

Meetings were held and much discussion ensued to put the description of the Shar-pei into a form that stressed this dog's unique qualities and abilities, one which English-speaking people could follow. Matgo Law, who, fortunately, possessed a more than adequate education and a knowledge of the English language, was elected to document this combined knowledge. This became the standard that accompanied his appeal to save the Shar-pei from extinction and is the one to which the American people responded. In all logic, then, it should be honored as the *only* standard for the breed, for one can't save a breed from extinction by changing the blueprint.

The plight of the Chinese Shar-pei in the early 1970's elicited a wave of varied response from dog fanciers. For some it was the challenge to help rescue a dying breed; for others it became a chance to line their pockets and fill their bankbooks. Many people who first answered Matgo's appeal had sincere intentions but lacked professional experience in dog breeding. Some were intrigued by the breed; many were speculators. Most of them at that time didn't realize, or comprehend, the purpose of a standard and failed to give it the importance that was warranted. Upon receiving their Shar-peis, these people accepted the dogs as they were, even though they were far from ideal representatives of the breed. They were limited in number and the faults were abundant. It would require a great deal of dedicated effort from the recipients of those first specimens to bring about the desired consistency described in the illustration that accompanied Matgo's article in *Dogs* magazine. The Shar-peis sent to the United States not only had visible flaws but many more genetic faults which were not readily apparent. Remember that these early specimens did not come from carefully planned breedings, so a great deal of research into the breed and perseverance to better the breed was required in order to eliminate flaws and produce worthy representatives.

I do not think there has ever been a perfect dog, and there probably never will be. The challenge in dog breeding lies in getting one's stock as close as possible to the standard of perfection. It was created, after all, as a guideline. Here is the first standard, written by Matgo Law, printed with the *Dogs* magazine article and sent along with those Shar-peis exported from China to the United States.

26

PROVISIONAL STANDARD OF THE
CHINESE SHAR-PEI

ORIGIN AND CHARACTERISTICS: This is a real Chinese breed which has existed for centuries in the southern provinces near the South China Sea. The original fountainhead is believed to be a town, Dah Let, in Kwun Tung Province. Dog fighting was the pastime of the farmers and small town dwellers since there was hardly any other form of entertainment then. The breed is equipped with all the features of a gladiator, features which will be mentioned point by point in the following structural descriptions. The very particular feature is the bluish-black tongue as seen in the Chow Chow. With the additions of the similar dignified expression and excellent guarding instinct, it is believed both the breeds come from the same origin. However, the Chinese Fighting Dog, as the breed was formerly called, is by no means a smooth-coated Chow Chow. They may have come from the same origin or, perhaps, the former descended from the latter.

In character, the Shar-pei is not a born fighter but will enjoy fighting if his owner encourages this tendency at an early age. Instead, he is a well-balanced dog with a dignified, scowling expression; loyal yet aloof; reserved in the presence of strangers while devoted to his family. He is prepared to sacrifice his own life for their survival. He does not need training; he is a natural, excellent household guard, and he is self-housebroken as a very young puppy.

GENERAL APPEARANCE: An active, compact, short- coupled dog. Well-knit in frame, giving a square build and standing firmly on the ground with the calm and firm stature of a formidable warrior.

HEAD AND SKULL: Skull flat and broad, rather large in proportion to the body, with little stop. Profuse and fine wrinkling appears on the forehead and cheeks and continues to form the heavy dewlaps. Muzzle is moderately long and broad from the eyes to the point of the nose (without any suggestion of tapering, but rather in the shape of a hippopotamus's mouth).

The muzzle on this specimen **(top, left)** is too long and narrow. Prick ears **(top, right)** are definitely a major fault according to the standard. A pup that holds his ears semi-erect usually turns out to be a prick-eared adult. Shir Du Sam Ku at four months **(bottom).** He has the type of head one likes to see on a puppy—good wide bone and small ears.

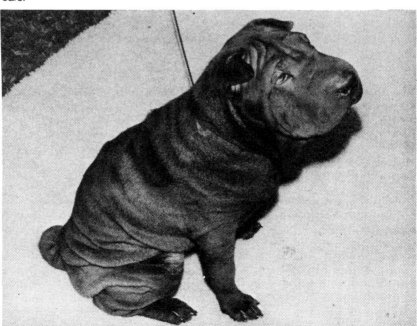

NOSE: Black, large, and wide. Occasionally there are cream dogs with brick-colored noses and light fawn dogs with self- colored noses, but a black nose is preferable.

EYES: Dark, small, almond-shaped, and sunken. Lighter colored eyes are found in cream and light fawn dogs. The small, sunken eyes are advantageous in dog fighting and reduce the chances of injury. Also, the sunken eyes and wrinkles upon the forehead help accentuate the scowling expression of the breed.

MOUTH: Teeth are strong and level, closing in a scissors bite. The canine teeth are somewhat curved (increasing the difficulty of freeing the grip). Tongue is bluish-black. Flews and roof of mouth are black. Gums preferably black.

EARS: Small and rather thick. Shaped like an equilateral triangle and slightly rounded at the tip. Set well forward over the eyes and wide apart. In contrast to the Chow Chow's ears, those of the Shar-pei should be set as tight to the skull and be as small as possible. This type of ear minimizes the opportunity of an opponent's getting a grip on the ears. Some specimens have ears so small (the size of a human thumbnail) that they just barely cover the ear burr.

NECK: Strong, full, set well on the shoulders with heavy folding skin and abundant dewlaps.

FOREQUARTERS: Shoulders muscular and sloping. Forelegs straight, of moderate length with good bones.

BODY: Chest broad and deep, back short; the lowest part of the backline is just behind the withers and rises to the loin. It is similar to the Bulldog but not as sunken as the latter. As with the wrinkles and dewlaps, there is a lot of skin-folding on the body. This abundance of loose skin allows the dog to turn and attack when gripped by his opponent.

HINDQUARTERS: Hind legs muscular and strong; hocks slightly bent and well let down, giving length and strength from loin to hock.

FEET: Moderate in size, compact, and firmly set; toes well split up with high knuckles, giving a firm stance.

TAIL: Thick and round at the base and evenly tapering to a fine point. There are three ways of carrying the tail: most desirable is the type set on top and curled tightly over to one side. Some tails are curled so tightly that they are in the shape of a small ringlet, the size of a large Chinese coin. The second type is curled in a loose ring. The third is carried high in a curve, not touching the back. This allows a dog to wriggle in a happier and more eager fashion. No matter what, the tail should be set high on the loin, showing the anus. The demand for a curling, tight tail is obvious—in fights, the tail between the legs is a sign of defeat.

COAT: Another peculiar feature of the breed. The coat is extremely short (shorter than a Bulldog's, which would be considered too long) and bristly; it is unusually harsh to the touch. It is a coat absolutely uncomfortable to be held in any canine mouth. The coat is not lustrous (as the coat of a Doberman Pinscher is), but by no means does it give the impression of being unhealthy looking.

COLOR: Whole colors [solid colors] such as black, fawn, light fawn, and cream are frequently shaded; for example, the underpart of the tail and back of thighs should be of a lighter color. These shadings should not be in patches or parti-colored.

WEIGHT AND SIZE: Around 18 to 20 inches at the withers, weighing 40 to 50 pounds. As in most breeds, the dog is heavier than the bitch and more squarely built.

FAULTS: Spotted tongue; a tail carried horizontally or covering the anus; a flat, long, shining coat; a tapering muzzle like a fox.

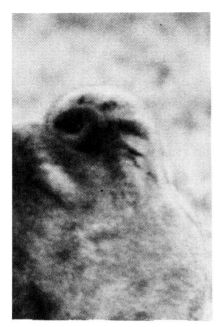

The three types of tail carriages desired: the tightly curled tail, set on top **(top, left);** the tail curled in a loose ring **(top, right);** and the curved tail carried high over the back without touching it **(bottom).**

31

 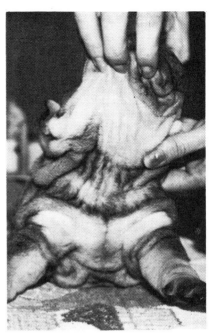

Black noses are preferred, according to the standard. This light-colored dog has a self-colored nose **(top, left)**. One should not mistake this pup as parti-colored **(top, right)**; on maturity, the colors will have blended together to produce sable. Down-Homes Mr. Universe has ears that are too large and set too low on the head **(bottom)**.

In April 1980, Mr. Law sent a more detailed description of the colors recognized in Hong Kong.

Chinese Shar-pei Color Varieties

Whole colors—black, red, deep fawn, light fawn, and cream frequently are shaded (the underpart of the tail and back of the thighs of a lighter color) but not in patches or parti-colored. This is what the standard says about colors: The Shar-pei should always be a solid color, never parti-colored. Shadings in the blacks and fawns are very common and not indicative of parti- colors. Parti-colors, brindle, and black-and-tans definitely should be penalized and certainly not used in breeding programs.

BLACK: Often shaded. Nose black from birth. Quite easily turns to a rusty-gray color in long exposure to sun.

FAWN: Deeper or lighter shade of cinnamon (color used to describe the Chow Chow in the United States). Often shaded. Born with a flesh-colored nose which turns black in about one week's time. Most common color.

RED: Also shaded, but not so distinctive as blacks and fawns. Nose black. Deep red color is not common.

CREAM: Shaded. Fawn ears and always associated with brick-colored nose with black rim (this is why this color is not termed "white"), but eye color should be deep brown and tongue color should be completely blue-black, as blue-black as that of the blacks and fawns.

DILUTE: Theoretically, cream is a dilute color, but the writer tried to distinguish the following described color variety from the "creams" and termed it "dilute."

The coat color is a deeper tone of reddish cream, the color of "hot cream" in the language of Persian cat breeders. The nose color is lighter brick-colored (lighter than the creams) without dark pigment around the rim. Eye color is usually lighter and the main difference is the tongue color, which is an overall shade of light purple instead of solid blue-black. If the overall color pattern is not diluted to an excessive degree, this color is acceptable.

Other Very Rare Colors

RUST: An overall rusty-gray (not a seasonal rusty-black color and much lighter overall color than the former). The intermixture of black and fawn hairs. Shaded. Darker along the top of the back. Rusty-fawn on the legs. The overall appearance of a whole [solid] color effect is maintained and no suggestion of distinctive border between darker and lighter color regions. Nose black.

CHOCOLATE: A whole [solid] chocolate color with a chocolate nose and yellowish eyes. Tongue color is light purple; it is whole [solid] colored, therefore acceptable. *Note:* The writer [Matgo Law] has so far seen only one specimen of this color, born from both black parents.

Except for those specially mentioned, the tongue color of all these color varieties should be completely blue-black, the stronger and deeper pigments being favored.

THE CHANGING AMERICAN STANDARD

The Chinese Shar-pei certainly is no longer in danger of becoming extinct, as we have already mentioned. Through sheer numbers the breed is well established. There *is* a danger of a different nature, however, and that is the possibility of the breed's original type, or conformation, being lost. Since the introduction of Matgo's standard in 1973, this document has undergone many changes. With each alteration made, Shar-pei type has become more variable.

In 1974 the Original Shar-pei Club was formed in the United States. In comparing the Shar-peis being imported from China to America with Matgo's standard, members of this newly- formed club noticed the lack of uniformity in the breed, i.e., disparities with regard to muzzles, tails, overall size, and so forth, so a new standard was drawn up to make allowances for these discrepancies. In fact, a letter was sent to members of the club, and it read

Sui Yeen's Firecracker of Bedlam **(top)**, owned by Ellen Weathers Debo. Down-Homes Oriental Pearl **(bottom)**, bred by Matgo Law of Hong Kong and imported and owned by Bedlam Kennels, displays a nice "meat mouth" so characteristic of the breed. Pearl is now owned by Go-Lo Kennels.

The ears should be small and rather thick, shaped like an equilateral triangle and slightly rounded at the tip. Additionally, they should lie flat against the head and be set wide apart, unlike the ears on this specimen **(top, left)**. These two pups are actually littermates, the smaller one reaching standard size upon maturity **(top, right).** She is Gold's Black Miracle of Bedlam, owned by Jim and Karen Wang. The tail carriage on this Shar-pei **(bottom)** is poor. A tail carried down, covering the anus or tucked between the legs, denotes cowardliness.

as follows: "Each owner must adopt, reject, or modify each sentence of the *general description,* based on the characteristics of their own Shar-pei, photos or features they have seen of other Shar-peis, and other Shar-pei knowledge they have." Instead of breeding out these faults and striving to produce dogs that conformed to the original standard from China, breeders incorporated the faults into their own breeding programs. The result was pink tongues, spotted tongues, various tail carriages (including brush tails, stub tails, and the complete absence of a tail), and lowered weight requirements to include dogs weighing 35 pounds. Apparently there was a misinterpretation of the letter written by Mr. Law concerning the tail, in which he wrote:

"TAIL: At the present stage, the Shar-pei's tail still varies. The type aimed at is always the one that is 'pulling' tightest towards the head. It represents his boldness, and in this respect it is still rated first in the order of the description. Natural bobtails and short tails crop up from litters (this is the exact same case with my own breeding) and at this stage they should not be deterred from the show ring. *But we should always breed towards the best."*

Some people felt that the Original Shar-pei Club was weak in organization and slow in the distribution of information, so another national club was formed in 1978, the Chinese Shar-pei Club of America, complete with a registry and a *third* standard. Further allowances were made for slightly turned-out pasterns, soft short coats, and soft long coats. Judges were instructed not to show personal preference for coat alone. Additional height was allowed (up to 22 inches) and weight was increased (to 60 pounds) to accommodate larger specimens. It should be mentioned that size can be controlled by breeding, not by diet or by altering the standard. For example, you can feed a Toy Poodle the most complete, nutritionally balanced diet possible, but I defy you to turn him into a Standard Poodle by such means. The genes set the size, not the food. To blame size increase on superior nutrition is ridiculous, and so is changing the Shar-pei standard to allow for these larger dogs.

The second club was short-lived and was eventually absorbed into the Original Shar-pei Club. On January 1, 1982, a revised standard provided for short coats (less than 1/2 inch) and brush coats (over 1/2 inch but under one inch), although short bristly coats were still preferred. Height ranged from 19 inches to 21 inches at the withers and weight ranged from 40 to 55 pounds. Although additional revisions are in the making, the standard presented by the Chinese Shar-pei Club of America in 1985 is as follows:

GENERAL APPEARANCE: An active, compact dog of medium size and substance. Square in profile, close coupled, the head somewhat large for the body. The short harsh coat, the loose skin covering the head and the body, and the typical muzzle shape imparts to the Shar-pei a unique individual stamp, peculiar to him alone. The loose skin and wrinkles are super-abundant in puppies but these features are less exaggerated in the adult.

HEAD: Large, proudly carried and covered with profuse and fine wrinkles on the forehead and cheek.

SKULL: Flat and broad, the stop moderately defined, the length from nose to stop is approximately the same as from stop to occiput.

MUZZLE: One of the distinctive features of the breed. It is broad and full with no suggestion of being snipey. The lips and top of muzzle are well-padded, causing a slight bulge at the base of the nose. When viewed from the front, the bottom jaw appears to be wider than the top jaw due to the excessive padding of the lips.

NOSE: Large and wide and darkly pigmented. Preferably black, but any color nose conforming to the general coat color of the dog is acceptable.

TEETH: Strong, meeting in a scissors bite, the canines somewhat curved.

EYES: Dark, extremely small, almond-shaped, and sunken, displaying a scowling expression. A somewhat lighter eye color is acceptable in lighter colored dogs.

According to the CSPCA breed standard, the muzzle should be broad and full, as is the case with this puppy **(top).** The youngster has what is referred to as a good, square "bone nose." A snipey nose, like that of a fox, is very undesirable in Shar-peis **(bottom).**

EARS: Extremely small, rather thick, equilateral triangles in shape, slightly rounded at the tips. They lie flat against the head and are set wide apart and forward on the skull with the tips pointing toward the eyes. The ears are not without erectile power, but a "prick ear" is a major fault.

TONGUE, ROOF OF MOUTH, GUMS, AND FLEWS: Solid bluish-black is preferred. Light purple or spotted (flowered) mouths are acceptable. A solid pink tongue is a major fault.

NECK: Medium length, strong, full, and set well into the shoulders. There are heavy folds of loose skin and abundant dewlaps about the neck and throat.

BACK: Short and close coupled. The topline dips slightly behind the withers, slightly rising over the short, broad loin.

CHEST: Broad and deep with the brisket extending to the elbow and rising slightly under the loin.

CROUP: Slightly sloping with the base of the tail set extremely high, clearly exposing a protruding anus.

TAIL: Thick and round at the base, tapering to a fine point, and curling over the back. No tail [i.e., the absence of a tail] is a major fault.

SHOULDERS: Muscular, well laid back and sloping.

FORELEGS: When viewed from the front, they are straight, moderately spaced, with elbows close to the body. When viewed from the side the forelegs are straight, the pasterns slightly bent, strong, and flexible. The bone is substantial but never heavy and is of moderate length.

FEET: Moderate in size, compact, well knuckled up and firmly set.

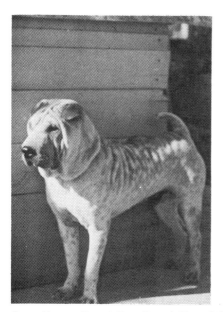

Down-Homes Sweet Pea **(top, left)** and Down-Homes Oriental Star **(top, right),** a cream female. Both of these Shar-peis were among the early dogs bred by Matgo Law of Hong Kong. Star is a daughter of Down-Homes Harmony. Down-Homes Don Kar in 1977, almost three years old **(bottom).** Matgo Law, breeder.

According to the standard, the Shar-pei head should be large and hippopotamus-shaped; the skull should be broad and flat, like that of Ch. Sterling's Rinky Ding **(top, left),** a two-year-old bred by Sterling Kennels. Ch. Bedlam's Panda and son, Oriental Treasure's Ugabee **(top, right).** Oriental Treasure's Put n on the Ritz, a ten-week-old female **(bottom).** All dogs on this page owned by Maryann Smithers of Oriental Treasure Kennel, Boonton, New Jersey.

42

DEWCLAWS: Removal of front dewclaws is optional. Hind dewclaws should be removed.

HINDQUARTERS: Muscular, strong, and moderately angulated, the hock well let down.

COAT: The extremely harsh coat is one of the distinguishing features of the breed. The coat is absolutely straight and off- standing on the main trunk of the body but generally lies somewhat flatter on the limbs. There is no undercoat. The coat appears healthy without being shiny or lustrous. A coat over one inch is a major fault. The Shar-pei is shown in as natural a state as is consistent with good grooming. The coat must not be trimmed in any way. A coat which has been trimmed is to be severely penalized.

COLOR: Solid colors. A solid-colored dog may have shading but not in patches or spots. A dog which is patched or spotted is a major fault.

GAIT: Free and balanced, with the rear feet tending to converge on a center line of gravity when the dog moves at a vigorous trot.

SIZE: Average height is 18 to 20 inches at the withers. Average weight is 35 to 55 pounds. The dog is usually larger and more square-bodied than the bitch but in either case should appear well-proportioned.

TEMPERAMENT: Alert, dignified, lordly, scowling, discerning, sober, and snobbish, essentially independent, and somewhat standoffish, but extreme in his devotion.

For more information on the Shar-pei, be sure to write to the Chinese Shar-pei Club of America, Inc., 55 Oak Court, Danville, California 94526.

ZL's Obie Wan Kenobi, owned by Dick and Zell Llewellyn of Shoestring Acres Kennel, Alvin, Texas.

44

Chapter 3

Shar-pei Kennels

This book just wouldn't be complete without mentioning some of the top kennels that are working hard to promote our beloved breed. If you are sincerely interested in the Shar-pei and in purchasing a fine representative, read about some of the kennels, go to dog shows in your area (where you can see firsthand the very finest Shar-peis being bred today), and write to the Chinese Shar-pei Club of America for names, addresses, and phone numbers of the breeders whose dogs you are interested in seeing and purchasing.

ALPHA REG.
by Michael Litz and Pamela R. Hurley
We first became interested in Shar-peis in 1978 when we saw one featured in *Dog World* magazine. At the time we were, and still are, raising Great Danes. We admit that the wrinkles are what caught our eye and made us curious to find out more about this unusual dog.

Our foundation bitch came from Ellen Weathers Debo in California; she was from a litter Ellen had received from a Canadian breeder who was not interested in raising or in placing the dogs. This bitch, Hurleys Shen Te Mi, is beautiful in body and movement; she has given us much soundness in our breeding program.

45

Ch. Moshu Shogun Gk. **(top),** owned by Pamela Hurley of Alpha Reg. Kennel, Monclova, Ohio. Hon. Ch. Boawnchein's Bilbo Baggins at four years old **(bottom).** Owners, Bob and Dawn Walling, Sunol, California.

We first bred for excellent fronts, rears, and movement, qualities we felt would win in any AKC ring. After breeding these qualities for three generations, we found a stud dog that could bring in the type we needed but that would not sacrifice the movement we had worked so hard to achieve. The dog who filled our needs was Best in Show Champion Shangri-las Gogorila Teabaggy by Best in Show Shir Du Bang.

Our accomplishments include: Champion Moshu Shogun of Gk., Champion Moshu Austi of Bruce Lee, Champion Gks Patrick of Bruce Lee, Champion Hoo Ji Tunzis Marmalade, Best in Show Champion Shangri-las Gogorila Teabaggy, Best in Show Champion Alpha Chanel Moshu, Champion Alpha Rogeans JD Hogg, Champion Alpha Ltd. Edition Crianca, and many more pointed on their way to championship.

Our foundation bitch, Hurleys Shen Te Mi, produced for us Best in Show Champion Alpha Chanel Moshu, Champion Moshu Shogun of Gk., and major-pointed Hurleys Dolly Parton Moshu, dam to Champion Moshu Austi of Bruce Lee. Hurleys Shen Te Mi is granddam to Champion Gks Patrick of Bruce Lee, Champion Moshu Chloe Whtdrgn Gk., Champion Whtdrgn Abracadabra Moshu, Champion Whtdrgn Airwolf, and Champion Whtdrgn Airiell. Our top producers have been Best in Show Champion Shangri-las Gogorila Teabaggy, Hurleys Shen Te Mi, Champion Moshu Shogun of Gk., and Hurleys Dolly Parton Moshu. We would like to add that Champion Chanel (Alpha Chanel Moshu) is the youngest Shar-pei in the breed to finish, finishing at six months and ten days of age at a very large Specialty show and going Best of Opposite Sex. The next time out at nine months of age Chanel went Best in Show over 20 champions-this makes three generations of Best in Show winners for Alpha Reg. Kennel.

Our goals and hopes for the Shar-pei are that the AKC recognizes us and that all breeders pull together to produce the perfect specimen.

BOAWNCHEIN

Bob and Dawn Walling of Sunol, California are the proud owners of Boawnchein Kennels. They became interested in Shar-peis after seeing photos of them in a children's magazine and started actively searching out the breed in 1976. At that time there were few Shar-peis to be found. Purchasing their first dog from the Es-haf Kennels in Cicero, Illinois in 1977, they bought a female from the same kennel a year later.

The kennel now houses Honorary Champion Boawnchein Bilbo Baggins, Honorary Champion Boawnchein Argie Fu Chew, Honorary Champion Tzo Tzo's Black Mushroom, and Boawncheins Ro-Duv-R-Do. Those dogs not quite finished but well on their way to championship titles are: Boawncheins Sesame O'Ken'One, Boawncheins Tic-Rish Von Kiper, Boawncheins Rosebud, and Boawncheins Char-coul of Lyn-Bar.

The Wallings' dogs have been involved with Jefferson Starship (a rock and roll group), whose video features a cream Shar-pei named "Sport." This dog was purchased from the Wallings by Don Nouello (otherwise known as Father Guido Sarduchi) of the television show "Saturday Night Live." One of San Jose, California's finest hotels uses the Boawnchein Shar-peis in their fashion shows. These dogs really are making a name for themselves!

Temperaments are not a problem at Boawnchein, and they are actively pursuing the elimination of hip dysplasia and eliminating those dogs known to carry skin problems. Dawn feels that the Shar-pei is becoming far more uniform as it grows in popularity.

BRUCE LEE'S

Bruce Lee's Chinese Shar-pei kennel is located in Oldwick, New Jersey. Established approximately six years ago, it is owned and operated by Bruce Lee Resnick. Bruce is one of those genuine hard-working go-getters. Not only has he succeeded in producing top-quality dogs that most kennels would be proud to claim, but he has also developed his kennel into a lucrative and profitable concern. He has helped promote the breed by having his dogs appear in numerous magazine articles and advertisements. Bruce started the kennel with dogs from almost every reputable source available at that time. Keeping those dogs from the top-winning, superior-producing, and trouble-free lines, Bruce went on to the next phase of his breeding program. Using only dogs that had been X-rayed and certified to be free of hip dysplasia, he also continued to upgrade the quality of the overall dog.

A Boawnchein dog **(top, left)** owned by Bob and Dawn Walling of Sunol, California. Boawnchein's To-Cu of Shor Joe **(top, right)** by Boawnchein's Argie Fu Chew out of Boawnchein's Attila Te Han. Bred by the Wallings. Bruce Lee's Invinceable at eight weeks **(bottom),** already showing potential. Bruce Lee Resnick of Oldwick, New Jersey, breeder.

Gold's Oriental Temple Bell in 1983 **(top, left)**. Like her dam, Pearl, she had convulsions and in early 1984 died of meningitis. Bred by Gayle and the late Marty Gold, Charlotte, North Carolina. Bill Morison's dog, Tai-Li of Tai-Li, **(top, right)** imported from China for use as foundation stock. Photo courtesy of Dick and Zell Llewellyn, Shoestring Acres, Alvin, Texas. Cho Sun Kennel's Dan Tsai **(bottom)**, a male pictured at two years of age. Breeder, J. P. Chan of Hong Kong.

Bruce Lee's kennel has the lead in producing champions, largely due to two of their outstanding stud dogs. One is Champion Gold's Black T.N.T. of Bruce Lee by House of Gold. OFA-certified, Dino, as he is called, is believed to have 25 champions to his credit and more in the making. He produces excellent movement and structure, and he passes on to his progeny a temperament that is truly delightful. Dino is a son of Bedlam Kennels's Shir Du Sam Ku, who is also behind a great many honorable champions and top-producing males.

Another very successful stud is Champion Gik's Patrick of Bruce Lee. He is a gorgeous copper red, and his services are in such high demand that he services from five to ten bitches every month. Bruce feels that Patrick is an excellent choice for daughters of Dino, each line complementing the other.

Bruce's goals remain the same—consistently working to weed out the problems and to help other breeders and newcomers to the breed in making the beautiful and challenging Shar-pei even better.

CHO SUN

Cho Sun Shar-pei is located in Hong Kong and is owned by J. P. Chan, who became interested in the breed in 1970, obtaining his foundation stock from Mr. L. Wing. Mr. Chan writes that they are breeding to true (original) Shar-pei form but not exaggerating it. He adds that the Hong Kong Kennel Club, although an affiliate of the London Kennel Club, has not made any effort to recognize the Shar-pei yet.

FINGERTAIL
by Jo Ann Webster

It is with great pleasure that I introduce myself as a breeder of Chinese Shar-peis through this book. In 1977 I met Ellen Weathers Debo while living in Yucaipa, California. I saw her dogs on a fun match bulletin cover and was absolutely intrigued by the uniqueness of the breed. I've always loved the show ring and have shown many breeds nationwide for 22 years. I had the feeling this new "wrinkled" breed of dog was going to be just what I wanted—the most unusual dog I've ever owned. Not knowing what I was really in for, I called Ellen and couldn't wait to see the rare dog she had imported from Hong Kong. My first impression of the Shar-pei was one of total awe—I just couldn't believe their faces and skin and their personalities. I wanted every one she owned and bought two of them, one of which became a champion producer and was my foundation brood bitch, Bedlam's Mortisha. One never forgets one's first attempts at breeding, and it was through Ellen that I had my start.

For the past seven years I have bred, raised, and shown several hundred Shar-peis. Many, many of my puppies and adults win through the O.S. at major shows and national Specialties. I have started many other breeders in Shar-peis and Fingertail Kennel is a name people know and recognize as quality Shar-peis that have those three characteristics towards which we all strive. Without the typical "meat mouth," sandy coat, and abundant wrinkling, our breed would not be set apart from other types of dogs. Soundness and type are what I breed for, and my dogs are known for this.

Through Mr. Ernest Albright I bought Tunzi's Peachy Keen. A good producer, she has whelped two champions and her puppies have won at many shows. Mr. Albright has adult dogs that retain a lot of wrinkling. I also have the Shir Du lines developed by Dugan Skinner. Mr. Skinner bred the most fabulous heads and mellow personalities I have ever come in contact with in our breed. He is also to be commended on his dedication to perfecting breed type. That Shir Du look is absolutely "stamped" into his line, and my best heads come from his dogs.

In my earlier days of breeding Shar-peis, my dogs had a lot of skin problems. I am happy to report that this is no longer the case.

The brush-coated Shar-peis seem to have stronger immune systems, and when they are crossed with short-coated dogs, the puppies have much better health and temperaments. Entropion has declined in my kennel but not totally bred out. I still have to tack puppies' eyes and have done over 200 puppies myself; the procedure, done at 21 days of age, is very easy. I've shown many vets what this has done. My goals are to breed a Shar-pei with all the characteristics of the breed. No other breed looks like the Shar-pei, and their unusualness is what attracts people to our breed. The Shar-pei's devotion to its owners is unbelievable!

Fingertail Golden Glo Ro Ro **(top)**, bred by Jo Ann Webster of Fingertail Kennel, Raritan, New Jersey. He is out of Tunzi's Peachy Keen. Four-month-old Fingertail Wu Jo **(bottom),** pictured "dropping" his puppy coat. Jo Ann Webster, owner.

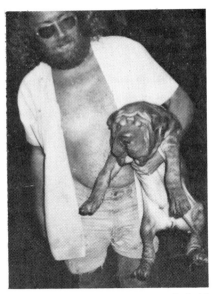

A seven-week-old Fingertail pup, Mandy **(top, left)**. This is not the proper way to hold a Shar-pei **(top, right)**. Support the dog with both hands, one being placed under the rear end. Down-Homes Prophet, at seven years, winning the Veteran's Class at a CSPCA show in 1984. Jo Ann and Duncan Redditt of Go-Lo Kennels, Alexandria, Virginia, owners.

I like our breed with a definite "hippo-head" type. In a breeding program you need type. I've done over 175 stud services and one must have a stud dog that can add the head the bitch just doesn't have, the loose skin everyone wants, and the bone and substance. All of my Shar-peis are OFA-certified and all are represented honestly.

Our breed certainly is the one that has made the biggest impression through newspapers, magazines, and television. I don't know of any other dog that has caused so much excitement! When I started in Shar-peis, there were 75 in the U.S.; now there are over 6,000 and the popularity is still growing, as our breed is in strong demand.

I was a national director for the Chinese Shar-pei Club of America for four years. Our breed club is probably the largest independent dog registry in the U.S. We have the largest Specialties of any breed being shown today.

GO-LO

Go-Lo Kennels is owned by Jo Ann and Duncan Redditt of Alexandria, Virginia. Jo Ann has owned, bred, and shown Lhasa Apsos, but she became intrigued with the Shar-pei one day and has loved and bred them ever since. Down-Homes Prophet was the first of her wrinkled companions, soon joined by Down-Homes Fortune Cookie. Within a year, three of the four puppies in her first litter had accumulated enough points to earn the title of Honorary Champion and one had earned her Companion Dog title in the obedience ring. This was the beginning of Go-Lo Kennels, so-named after her husband, Duncan. He has worked with the Chinese community in Washington, D.C. for over 20 years, and they fondly call him "Go-Lo," which in Chinese translates to "tall man"—an apt name for his six-foot-eight-inch frame.

Jo Ann helped to organize the Mid-Atlantic Chinese Shar-pei Club and served as its president for two years. In 1983 she assumed her current role as editor and publisher of *The Orient Express 11*, the breed magazine for the Chinese Shar-pei, which serves as a voice for the breed. It expresses the concerns about the Shar-pei's future and features articles from other breeders, veterinarians, and the like.

Restrained by lack of space, she limits her breeding program to one litter a year. For the time being, her major contribution to the Chinese Shar-pei is to dispense information about the breed.

HOUSE OF GOLD

The House of Gold Kennels in Charlotte, North Carolina was owned and operated by the late Marty Gold and his wife, Gayle. Marty had high hopes and a driving ambition to have the very best Shar-peis; he was dedicated to the breed and worked very hard to promote and establish the dogs. Gayle is now taking up where Marty left off, determined to bring Marty's dreams to reality by breeding only the best to the best and producing superior Shar-peis.

First becoming interested in the breed after seeing pictures in 1973, they spent a few years actively searching for the "right" Shar-pei. Marty had his heart set on a black; it also had to have a good, black tongue, a full tail, and good ears. In November of 1979, they found her, Fond of Lao Te, at the Gremminger's Tzo Tzo Kennels.

When "Ming," as she was affectionately called, was of "marriageable" age, she was flown to Bedlam Kennels, California, to join up with Shir Du Sam Ku. They produced a litter of three males, one of which became Champion Gold's Rising Sun. The results from the breeding were so impressive that it was repeated, this time producing an all-black litter of four males and three females from which came Champion Gold's Black T.N.T. Bruce Lee and Champion Gold's Black Magic. These two dogs have produced close to 50 champions. The rest of the litter was not shown, but from the sisters have also come champions.

House of Gold has owned or bred 18 champions to date and has five others with major points. All dogs in the kennel are champions. Champion Gold's Chu Tien of Borden, siring only two litters, has two champions to his credit.

Gayle's goals are to breed a healthier dog with fewer problems and sound movement. She is one among many who expresses the wish that the breed does not become exploited. Gayle, as did her husband, truly loves this breed and feels it has a great deal to offer. In a few short years this kennel has come so far.

56

Two generations represented here from the House of Gold: Ch. Gold's Black Magic **(top)** and Fond of Lao Te **(bottom),** Magic's dam and the Gold's foundation bitch. Owners, Gayle and the late Marty Gold, Charlotte, North Carolina.

Tsihmao's Kung Kung and Tsihmao's Kang Yu Wei, brothers, bred by Linda Reinelt of Suderau, West Germany **(top).** Tsihmao's Chin-Se **(bottom),** bred by Ms. Reinelt.

HOUSE OF TZO-TZO
by Jo Ann Gremminger

I first became interested in the Chinese Shar-pei in 1976 after seeing an article in *Dog Fancy* magazine. I called the author of the article, Mr. Ernest Albright, and a couple of weeks later I had my foundation bitch, Albright's Woo Ya Rook. Over the next year I got another female from Dee Seas, Down-Homes Ip Moon Chee, a Chinese import. I also got a fawn male from Lisette Offergeld and a black male named Gong Bo Ding of Eshaf from Vern Fahse. In September of 1977 Bo Ding was bred to Yu Hu, owned by Pat Pagnard, and I acquired Yu Mi-Te-Man of Tzo Tzo who turned out to be one of the outstanding show dogs and stud dogs for several years. Mi-Te-Man took his first points at the C.S.P.C.A. Specialty in 1980 by going Best of Breed over several champions from the 6-9 Puppy Class. Over the next three years he won numerous Bests of Breed, Group wins, and Best in Show wins. He retired in 1983 after going Best of Breed at the South Central Specialty in Houston. His soundness of temperament and movement made him a consistent winner all across the country under many judges. He had sired many C.S.P.C.A. champions and his get are now producing quality Shar-pei. Mi-Te-Man typifies the soundness of temperament, structure, and movement I have always tried to produce.

My hope for the future of the breed is that the breeders do not lose sight of the importance of quality and soundness in their breeding programs or get wrapped up in the financial gains to be made and forget what the Chinese Shar-pei stands for.

KUNG FU

Located in Hamburg, Germany, this kennel is owned by Joachim Weinberg. Joachim himself filled us in on the particulars of his kennel's background:

> I am the president of the club Fur Exotische Rassehunde (rare dogs) that includes the Shar-pei. In 1978, I imported the first Shar-peis to Europe, Bedlam's Lover Boy and Bedlam's Love Song. In Luxembourg Bedlam's Lover Boy became the first Shar-pei champion in the world. I started the breed in partnership with Linda Reinelt, and we

imported Down-Homes Cream Zulu from Mr. Law's kennel in Hong Kong. The first two litters were the result of our working partnership, and then Miss Reinelt and I separated.

I am proud to say that I made it possible for the Shar-pei to be recognized by the FCI along with an interim standard. We can now show the breed and they are able to receive the national championship title, although we will have to wait for the international title a while longer.

There are now about 200 Shar-peis in Germany. Down-Homes Cream Zulu was a very important stud in the German Shar-pei scene. His imported brother, Down-Homes Zambo, is now in Switzerland and has his obedience titles.

I am a judge for the entire Toy group and part of the Non-Sporting group. I have judged in 15 countries, including the United States, Australia, Italy, Denmark, and Finland. My breeding goals for the Shar-pei are to achieve the cobby, sturdy body type; the meat mouth; the straight front; the good bones; the solid blue-black tongue; the correct short, harsh coat (or the shortest brush coats); the correct tail set; and the sound movement.

LOONG CH'AI

Loong Ch'ai Kennel, Sarasota, Florida, is fortunate to have Betsy Davidson and her husband, Red, as owners-breeders. Betsy is a very dedicated lady, working extremely hard to weed out problems in the Chinese Shar-pei. Appointed by the Chinese Shar-pei Club of America as OFA representative for the breed, she takes the job to heart. Her convictions of weeding out hip problems are strictly adhered to in her own kennel.

Betsy writes that after being bewitched by display ads in *Dog World* magazine, a Shar-pei puppy on the Betty White television show was the clincher. She continues, "In the summer of 1980, we saw our first living, breathing, plushy, mush-faced adult, accompanied by—oh, bliss!—her five puppies who had just turned three weeks old. Nearly four months passed before one of these

Germany's first imported Chinese Shar-peis, Bedlam's Lover Boy and Bedlam's Love Song, pictured with Linda Reinelt and Joachim Weinberg in 1979 **(top).** Tsihmao's Kang Yu Wei **(bottom),** owned by Linda Reinelt, Suderau, West Germany.

61

Three-month-old Loong Ch'ai's Midnight Special, a Ch. Gold's Black Magic grandson and a Shir Du Sam Ku great-grandson **(top, left).** Betsy Davison, breeder. Fingertail Wu Jo of Loong Ch'ai at eight weeks **(top, right).** By Boawnchein's Indigo Ro Ro out of Bedlam's Mortisha. Owner, Loong Ch'ai Kennel. Maryann Smithers's young Oriental Treasure's Honey at three weeks **(bottom).**

babes became our Sui Yeen's Loong Nu (Dragon Daughter)."

Loong Nu was approaching her first birthday when the Davidsons acquired a handsome black male; he had small, well-placed ears and a mouth as black as the outside of him. Although the breeding was successful and the resulting nine pups were beautiful, tragedy awaited. Most of the pups had demodectic mange and were dysplastic. Betsy then set out to learn as much as she could about hip dysplasia. The second time the bitch was bred it was to a stud with OFA-certified "good" hips. His dam was OFA-certified excellent, and his sire was X-rayed excellent. His name was Gold's Black Magic. Alas, this also was not a simple, easy pregnancy. Loong Nu developed malabsorption (it was thought then to be a problem with low levels of thyroid but had been caused by a protein anemia and other deficiencies). Throughout the pregnancy she was sick with diarrhea and suffered loss of appetite. She delivered two pups, then developed uterine inertia and five male pups were delivered by C-section. They were tiny (6-7 ounces— normal weight being close to 16 ounces or better); five died over the next three days. Although the remaining two had good hips, they developed other problems and had to be put down at five months and a year respectively.

In April of 1982, Betsy and Red acquired Oriental Temple Belle, a beautiful fawn bitch who, at six months, entered her first show and came away with a five-point major. Belle's preliminary hip X-rays were also disappointing, and she was spayed. Her replacement was Gold's Magic Moment. In 1983, Loong Ch'ai Ho-Ghee Poon was acquired. Both of these dogs have sound hips and a breeding is soon to take place. A little female, Lu Ch'ai Star Dust Melody, has had a preliminary X-ray, which was excellent, at six months.

Betsy's goals are to breed sound dogs with good hips, good eyes (with nothing more than puppy tacking), no demodectic mange, and no stop infections. She also plans to eventually eliminate hip dysplasia in her Shar-peis. She feels indiscriminate breeding is one of the worst problems the breed faces, and she does her best to educate people about the pitfalls of the breed and tries to comfort the others who have been devastated by Shar-pei ills. To quote Betsy, "It is a difficult breed but so rewarding to live with that we don't want to raise any other."

ORIENTAL TREASURE

The Oriental Treasure, located in Boonton Township, New Jersey, is owned by Maryann Smithers, who competes in both the breed and obedience ring. Her two German Shepherd Dogs and Poodle have their Companion Dog titles, and one has a Companion Dog Excellent title. The Chinese Shar-pei is the first breed that Maryann has seriously shown in the breed ring. To date she has trained and finished six to their championship, four of which she herself owns.

The Oriental Treasure's first champion was Bedlam's Panda, and she was also the first to get her Companion Dog title. Panda started her winning tradition at three-and-a-half-months at her first show by taking Best Puppy at the Long Island Rare Breed Show. Panda's first Best of Breed was at six months at Mid-Island Kennel Club under judge Robert Montheard. At ten months, at the New Jersey Dog Federation show, she took Best of Breed over 19 Shar-peis and then went on to win the AKC Non-Sporting Group First under Ray Swidersky. In March of 1981, at the Southeast Chinese Shar-pei Specialty, under an AKC judge and with an entry of 35, Panda took Best of Breed and the next day took Best of Opposite Sex. On July 10, 1982 at the Hudson Valley Rare Breed Show, under Norman Shuman, Panda added another rosette for Best of Breed. Panda again won Best of Breed on October 23, 1983, at the Delaware Valley Kennel Club under AKC judge Rose Molder. Her latest and maybe the most impressive win was September 23, 1984 at the Akita Club of the Delaware Valley. Panda, handled by Vicki Izzo, placed first in Junior Showmanship competition. Then, with Maryann handling, she won her second leg for her C.D. title and went on to win Best of Breed and Best in Show with Vicki Izzo handling. Panda has many more Bests of Breed and Bests of Opposite Sex to her credit, but keep in mind that she took time out to have three litters of puppies.

Panda is a terrific producer and a wonderful mother, having had seven puppies in her first litter and nine each in the second and third litters. Her first litter produced Maryann's first homebred champion, Oriental Treasure's Honey. At one-and-a-half years, Honey has a Group First, two Bests of Breed and four Bests of Opposite Sex. Honey was not campaigned because she whelped a

Oriental Treasure's Cashew pictured at eight months **(top),** owned by Georgia and Vicki Izzo. Oriental Treasure's Joy, a seven-week-old puppy, bred by Maryann Smithers of Boonton, New Jersey **(bottom).** Cashew was also bred by Maryann.

An Oriental Treasure eight-week-old female puppy **(top)** bred by Maryann Smithers of Boonton, New Jersey and owned by Cynthia Kehoe. Oriental Treasure's All That Jazz **(bottom)** at two months old, bred and owned by Maryann.

litter of five which gave Maryann Oriental Treasure's X tra Trouble. Trouble, at six months old, has a Best in Show and two Best Puppy awards to her credit.

Panda's second litter gave us Champion Oriental Treasure's Put N on the Ritz, known as Skeeder, and Oriental Treasure's All that Jazz. Skeeder's best win was at seven months when she took her first points and Best of Breed over 32 Shar-peis, including champions, under AKC judge Ruth Terry. Jazz has won three Best Puppy awards and three Winners Bitch awards.

In the summer of 1984, Panda whelped another litter, giving Maryann another Best in Show winner, known as Oriental Treasure's Xavier owned by Georgia Izzo. Xavier's most impressive win was under judge Richard Tang at the Chinese Shar-pei Club of the Northeast Specialty where he won Best in Show Junior Puppy.

Maryann attributes the quality of her Shar-peis to a carefully-planned breeding program, with her main concerns being temperament, straight fronts, and terrific movement. Every bitch at Oriental Treasure is bred with the intention of producing better dogs, and it is important to breed dogs that complement one another rather than base the breeding on pedigrees alone.

SHIR DU

Wolcottville, Indiana is the home of this very well-known kennel owned by Shirley and Dugan Skinner. They obtained their original stock from California, Ohio, and imported from Hong Kong. Dugan writes, "We have been able to increase muzzle size and at the same time produce a more square build in our dogs. We definitely have improved personality and developed far better temperaments. Among the top studs at the kennel are Shir Du Ling Fu, Shir Du Mr. Bob, Shir Du Pack-Kee, and Shir Du Clyde. Our top girls are Foo-z, Shir Du Char Min, Shir Du Kan Tung, Yen Se, Shir Du Chass Tee, Cher, Shir Du Dusk-Kee, and Shir Du Val."

Shir Du Sam Ku

Shir Du Sam Ku is one of the best known and quite possibly one of the top contributing stud dogs to date. Sam is often in the pedigrees of dogs that have earned the title of Honorary Champion and those being campaigned in the ring working for that title. He is also behind many stud dogs who, in turn, are producing puppies of superior quality.

On a particularly bleak and miserable day, Sam's picture arrived in the mail. That picture made me temporarily forget my problems and laugh. I had to have him!

Perhaps this will serve as my tribute to Sam who has been a constant source of pleasure and reliability for eight years. He's been there through life's little ups and downs, when friends and family died, moved away, or relationships ended. Sam has been at my side comforting and protecting me. His intelligence and intuition are a source of constant amazement. By choice he is a man's dog, preferring the company of my husband, Phil. He likes to feel that a woman's place is in the home where she caters to his needs; in fact, he greets me with a scowl and a throaty rumble when he feels I've been gone longer than necessary. When I do actually leave for a few days, I'm greeted on my return with little love nips and a wagging body (his tail is so tightly curled that it can't be wagged!) This is about the only time that Sam ever loses his rather "aloof" manner and lets me know I've been missed.

An AKC judge once said of Sam, "You are aware of his presence when he enters a room or walks into a show ring." His contribution to the world of Shar-peis is well known, as he has produced champions both in the United States and abroad. Sam has some very dominant traits; he has improved heads, curled tails, and reduced ear size.

SHOESTRING ACRES

Shoestring Acres of Alvin, Texas is owned by Dick and Zell Llewellyn. They first became interested in the Chinese Shar-pei early in 1978 when their daughter Christina brought home a picture of the two puppies featured in *National Geographic World*. Obtaining their foundation stock from Mr. Ted Linn, of Linn's Kennels, and Mr. William Morrison, in six years of breeding they have not only been able to improve the type and soundness of their stock but have fortunately had only minor eye problems and no major skin problems of any sort.

Breeding stock is selected for the shortest, harshest coats possible and for a high degree of intelligence. All breeding stock is X-rayed before being used to make sure that individuals are free of

Eight-year-old Shir Du Sam Ku **(top)** showing good wrinkle retention as an adult. Bred by Shirley and Dugan Skinner of Shir Du Kennel, Wolcottville, Indiana and owned by the author. Shir Du Ling Fu at seven years **(bottom),** bred by the Skinners.

69

Hon. Ch. Gold's Rising Sun **(top)** and Hon. Ch. ZL's Dallas Delight **(bottom),** both owned by Dick and Zell Llewellyn, Shoestring Acres, Alvin, Texas.

hip dysplasia. If a better quality pup is not then produced, it is spayed or neutered, and the Llewellyns go back to the drawing board and try again.

Shoestring Acres has produced many dogs that have won the title Honorable Champion. Linn's Ping is the first Shar-pei in the national club to have received both the conformation and obedience awards. Zl's Cinnamon Cricket is also an obedience champion. Top studs at the present time are Champion Gold's Rising Son and Zl's Obie Wan Kenobi. Unfortunately the Llewellyns recently suffered the loss of Zl's McTavish who produced superior-type puppies. Gold's Rising Son and Zl's Cinnamon Cricket teamed up to produce an extremely fine dog, Zl's Fito Bandito of Tex. He was acclaimed as one of the finest examples of the breed at the world show in Madrid, Spain. His accomplishments include eight C.A.C.'s, seven C.A.C.I.B.'s, eight Bests of Breed, and an Excellent 1.

Producing puppies of excellent quality is a way of life at Shoestring Acres. Zell is an excellent handler who loves to show her dogs. She is anxious for AKC recognition, as then she may compete where she feels it really counts; her wish is that the breed not be ruined by careless breeders before it has a chance to prove itself. Her goals are someday to color breed, believing that this would help to purify and set color. At the moment this goal is taking a back seat to the more important conformation breeding program. The other goal at Shoestring Acres is perfection, and as Zell says, "that perfect puppy will always be in the next litter."

THREE SISTERS
by June Collins

I first became interested in the Chinese Shar-pei in the early 1970's when I saw a photograph of one in a Vancouver newspaper. The dog was owned by a Chinese gentleman there, and it was described as a Chinese Fighting Dog, the only one in Canada. No more details were given. That picture hung on my wall for several years and finally disappeared both from the wall and my mind.

In 1977 in San Diego, unable to sleep after a Fourth of July celebration, I was up in the early hours idly perusing the Classified Ads in the *Los Angeles Times*. The ad read: "Chinese Fighting Dog" and carried a phone number in Arkansas. I was barely able to put the paper down and couldn't believe my good fortune. As soon as it was a reasonable hour in Arkansas, I called the number and was able to reserve a puppy, one of two females. The breeder was very wary of me, it seemed, and I was to learn some six years later that because I responded so quickly, she thought I was a dog-fighting enthusiast. Several months later, after numerous calls back and forth, I was finally allowed to pick up my puppy at the Los Angeles airport. The dog was Yuk Lan, an extremely short-coated, spirited female who was to become the most important creature in my life, bar none, for six-and-one-half years. She was by Down-Homes Ginger Guts ex Down-Homes Frumpy, both imported from Hong Kong's Matgo Law.

Two years later, after apparently having passed some sort of "eligibility test," I travelled to Arkansas to pick up two more females by Dragon Lady's Jess of Gun Club ex Down-Homes Frumpy. These two "ladies" were as different as night and day and were the only two in the litter. While Ming had the coloration and body type of their half-sister, Yuk Lan, Ruby was the more beauteous, being a deadringer for their maternal grandsire, Down-Homes Bobby.

I had made numerous attempts to breed Yuk Lan around this time and had not had any luck. She took an aversion to the two males, who were very nice and within driving range, and wore all of us out with her high-mindedness. Finally I shipped four of my assorted dogs to a boarding kennel, brought a stud dog into my home for a week, and the job was done!

Meanwhile, I had become so enamored of this particular line of Shar-pei that I was overjoyed when the Arkansas breeder called to tell me that I could come to her summer retreat in Canada and pick out a male puppy from a newly-born litter of eight puppies by Dragon Lady's Jess of Gun Club out of Yuk Lan's full sister, Ming Sui. The puppies were all the same exquisite shade of fawn, and all had super-short coats. I chose the male with the most massive head and sweetest disposition; this was Ah Chong, now four years old and a very fine fellow who takes his role of stud dog very seriously. Four months after Ah Chong was born, Yuk Lan had her first litter, by Down-Homes Union Jack, and out of the four puppies, I realized that one was truly outstanding. Although I did not need another stud dog since I had Ah Chong, I decided to

Matgo Law chats with the well-known and respected AKC judge, Mr. Vincent Perry, on his visit to the United States **(top, left).** Two generations of Three Sisters breeding: Three Sisters' Jakie **(top, right)** at five months, and her sire, Three Sisters' Ah Dah, at four years **(bottom).** Owner, June Collins.

Matgo Law's most important foundation bitch **(top, left)**. She has an excellent head but poor ears, in terms of what is called for in the standard. Down-Homes Black Pearl **(top, right),** on the other hand, has not only an excellent head, but the correct ear set. Down-Homes Little Pea **(bottom)** was in whelp when she was exported from Hong Kong to the United States. Owned by Lois Alexander.

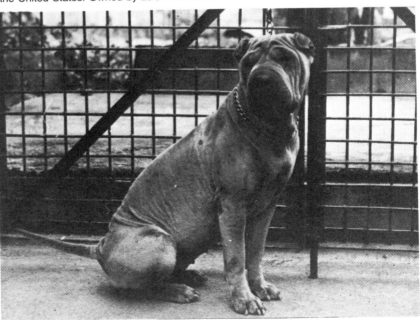

trust my budding instincts and kept this impressive little fellow who was to be known as Three Sisters' Ah Dah, which means "something special."

It occurred to me that since I liked my strain of Shar-pei very much (because they all had beautiful coats, black tongues, and, for the most part, very good heads, as well as robust health and some beautiful ancestors) I would try to produce Shar-peis with all of these specific qualities—especially the good head types found in my line—so I began to study the pros and cons of linebreeding. I was especially fascinated with evidence that dogs so closely resembling their ancestors had already been produced in this line—Ruby was indeed Bobby's granddaughter, and Ah Dah most certainly was cut from Down-Homes Un Long's cloth, although he also bore a spooky resemblance to his paternal grandsire, Clown-Nosed Buddha. And Ming Jeu, poor lass, had developed into almost a clone of her paternal granddam, the Dragon Lady, especially in the ear department. Ming had semi-prick ears, but since she had a very well-developed body and superior good health, I felt that her ears would simply be put on the negative side of the ledger and would be just one of those features to try and breed out. She had, among other good features, a poker-straight front, which she has passed on to all but a few of her 20 puppies.

In the seven-year history of Three Sisters' Kennels, there have been nine litters using just my own related stock. We have produced 34 puppies: all but three had extremely short coats; all but two were fawns, the exceptions being creams with black points; and 21 had exceptional or better-than-average large heads. There have been no reports of structural problems, such as hip dysplasia or subluxating patellae, or less-than-perfect bites. There have been five spotted tongues, one elongated soft palate requiring surgery, two known hypothyroid dogs with attendant skin problems, and two dogs with demodex. There have been no spotted puppies.

We have had no record in the show ring to elaborate on, except for Ruby's placing first in Open Bitch at the St. Louis National and Ah Dah's placing second at the National in Portland in Bred-By-Exhibitor Class, and these are the only two major shows where we have shown dogs. Ah Chong has sired two Honorable Champions when bred to a superior outside bitch, Charming Wun of Paradise, owned by Carol Gorman. We also have not entered into Obedience.

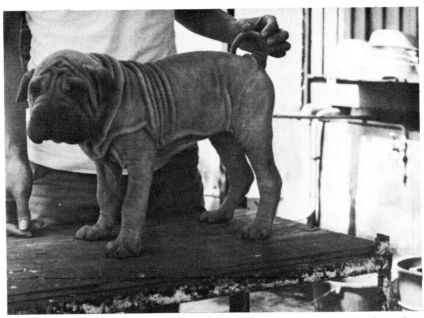

Down-Homes Frumpy at 12 weeks **(top)**. Bred by Matgo Law and owned by the author. Eight-year-old Down-Homes Jade Ming, also bred by Matgo Law, now owned by the Skinners (Shir Du Kennel) of Wolcottville, Indiana **(bottom)**.

Joe Gonzales's Bedlam's Cindy.

My goals for the future are to continue my linebreeding program, with occasional outcrossing, in hopes of producing puppies which will consistently feature the head types of Ah Chong *or* Ah Dah, the coat type of Ming Jeu *or* Ah Chong, the excellent eyes of Ruby *or* Ah Chong, the body type of Ah Dah, the straight front of Ming Jeu *or* Ah Chong and Ruby, the beautiful strong and massive body of Ah Dah, the ears of Ruby, and the superior good health of all of these. I would also like to preserve the sweet temperament of Ruby and Ming, and also Ah Chong, and the extreme devotion of Ah Dah, but without the aggressiveness.

My hope for the breed in the future is that we do not stray too far from the essence of the breed; that of a short-coated, black-tongued dog with small ears set tightly to the head; with a well-curled tail carried up and over the back; with good, healthy eyes and beautiful expression on a proportionately large head; an intelligent, watchful dog devoted to his family and turf. He should be a wrinkled dog, but not to the extent that his wrinkles pose a health problem, nor should his wrinkles be the result of a health problem. I hope that breeders will move forward in moderation and place emphasis on good health and temperament, as well as on definitive features, for a Shar-pei with excellent type is of little value if it can't see, can't stand up or run, and lives only a few years.

77

A Shar-pei's nails grow at an alarming rate. Start trimming them when your dog is young so that it will become accustomed to the procedure, and be careful not to cut the quick.

Chapter 4

Grooming and Good Health

The grooming of your Shar-pei is definitely not much of a chore. Since his coat is like sandpaper, he will not get tangles, pick up burrs, or shed on your furniture and clothes (at least not to a noticeable degree) the way other dog breeds do; however, he does require some attention to keep him clean, comfortable, and smelling sweet so that he is nice to be near.

A regular grooming program will help keep your pet healthy and happy. It allows you to keep close tabs on your Shar-pei's general health and enables you to observe and take fast action on small problems before they become serious.

A good bristle brush will whisk away the dust from his coat and stimulate his circulation. *Never* use a wire brush on the short, bristled coat, as it will scratch and tear the skin.

BATHING

Your Shar-pei may require an occasional bath, using warm water and a good-quality shampoo made for dogs. If he has skin problems, a medicated shampoo may be needed, which can be obtained from your veterinarian. Start at the back of the head and work towards the tail. Exercise care in keeping the shampoo out of his eyes and the water out of his ears. Some people prefer to put a few drops of mineral oil in the eyes and cotton in the ears as a precautionary measure. Wipe his face clean with a warm, wet cloth. Be sure to rinse him thoroughly; then rinse again, as some shampoos may be irritating if left on the skin. Be sure to dry him well so that he won't catch cold.

Baths should be given in moderation, since they tend to wash away the natural oils that protect the skin. If his skin is dry and flaky, a final rinse with a skin softener, such as Alpha Keri, should help. In extreme cases of dryness, oils may need to be added to the diet. Check with your veterinarian first, but I find that Linitone, corn oil, and bacon fat work well. If the dog's feces become too loose, cut down immediately on the quantity of oil fed. Again, ask your vet for advice on diet supplements to treat skin dryness or other skin disorders.

EARS

Since the Shar-pei standard calls for small, tight ears, frequent attention must be given to them. With a tight ear, there is a lack of air circulation and the ears become susceptible to ear mites and infection. Check the ears once a week and clean them gently with a cotton swab moistened with baby oil or a solution of equal parts of water and 3% hydrogen peroxide. Do not probe too deeply into the ear. If you find a dark, waxy discharge, your pet probably has ear mites. A yellowish color and bad odor may indicate severe infection. In either case, get help from your veterinarian.

A sore ear left unattended will be a real misery for your dog. In extreme cases it can cause disfigurement. His way of letting you know he has an ear problem may be by hanging his head to one side, by shaking his head repeatedly, or by scratching at and behind the ear. Constant scratching at the ear may lead to a hematoma, which is the breaking of blood vessels; the ear flap then fills with blood, creating a large swelling. In most cases this will require surgical treatment.

Routine ear care is important so that if problems arise they can be treated promptly.

EYES

Keep a careful watch on your dog's eyes. Even those puppies that show no sign of entropion may develop the condition at a later age. Eye entropion, sadly, is a very common problem in the

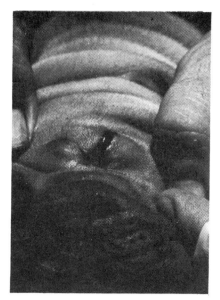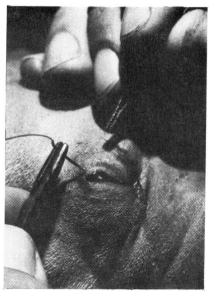

You can see how tightly the eyelids roll in **(top, left)** when entropion is present. The excess wrinkling around the eyes causes this to happen in Shar-peis, and the usual procedure is to remove a piece of skin parallel to the edge of the eyelid. The incision is then closed with several sutures **(top, right)** using a small curved needle, and the knot is tied tightly and pulled away from the edge of the eyelid **(bottom).**

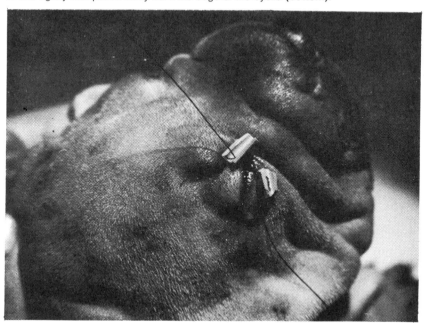

This little fellow, a three-week-old, should have his eyes open by now. He is afflicted with eye entropion, which can cause a dog great discomfort **(top).** Six-week-old fawn female pups, out of Bedlam's Mortisha by Chini Chipper Fingertail, owned by Jo Ann Webster of Fingertail Kennel, Raritan, New Jersey **(bottom).** Chewing on a large knuckle bone helps keep the teeth in good condition.

Chinese Shar-pei. It is an inrolling of the eyelid (either top or bottom, although frequently both eyelids are involved). These inrolled lids bring the eyelashes into direct contact with the cornea and create great discomfort, making it necessary for the animal to blink constantly. Entropion afflicts other dog breeds, but in Shar-peis it is caused primarily by the excess of wrinkling on the face and around the eyes. Some Shar-pei lines are more susceptible than others. Of course the breeding of deep-set eyes, as called for in the standard, only compounds the problem. Some puppies are unable to open their eyes at 10 to 14 days as they should.

Minor forms of entropion may be caused by dust or debris collecting in the eye, by eyelashes growing in the wrong direction, or by eye injury. If caught at the outset, this temporary form of entropion can be treated by administering the correct eye salve or ointment as prescribed by the vet. It is important to keep the eyes clean, using *warm* water only and, occasionally, Liquid Tears. Any sign of discharge from the eyes, rubbing of the eyes with the paws, or continual blinking should be reported at once to your veterinarian.

A large percentage of Shar-pei puppies have their eyelids rolled out and tacked in place for about two weeks. This procedure provides relief from the pain, and quite often it gives the wrinkling around the eyes enough time to smooth out as the puppy grows into his skin. In severe cases, surgery is required. A small piece of skin is removed from either or both of the problem eyelids, then closed and sutured—rather like taking a tuck in a garment. Some Shar-peis need several of these operations because as they grow, they become more wrinkled.

Entropion should never be left to take care of itself. If left untreated, the condition could cause sore watery eyes, infection, ulcers on the cornea, and even blindness.

MOUTH

The Shar-pei's mouth also needs attention. Those individuals with large, fleshy mouths, whereby even the lips have folds, need special care. Food gets trapped between these folds and becomes rancid, producing a foul odor. After your Shar-pei has finished his meals, carefully stretch his lips and gently clean out and thoroughly dry these areas. Should there already be signs of redness, apply a light dusting of cornstarch. If this doesn't help, ask your veterinarian to provide you with something safe to use on and around the dog's mouth.

Not only do the overly-padded lips trap food, but they push against the bottom teeth (causing overshot mouths) and cover the teeth while the dog chews his food (a source of discomfort for him). At times he even bites through his own lips, since they get in the way. Check in and around his mouth regularly.

TEETH

If you feed your dog soft foods, it is important to supplement this offering with hard biscuits, dry kibble, and one of the various Nylabone® products while he is still a puppy. These chewing aids help divert him from gnawing on your feet, your shoes, your furniture, and so on. Nylabones, especially, keep a dog's teeth strong and healthy. Unlike other dog bones on the market today, Nylabones do not splinter or fall apart. Instead, they will last indefinitely, and as they frill, they become doggie toothbrushes that clean and massage the gums.

Even though you supply your Shar-pei with hard chew items, tartar may build up on the teeth, especially as the dog ages. For this condition, you will have to seek the help of your veterinarian, who will scale the dog's teeth periodically so as to keep them in good working order.

FEET

Occasionally feet are wrinkled on some Shar-peis, and many of these dogs experience soreness between the toes and inside the foot pads. Try to keep your dog off damp surfaces as much as possible. Medicated powder used to treat athlete's foot can be lightly applied to the problem areas and works quite well. Lack of exercise is another reason a dog may chew and lick his feet, and the moisture from the mouth can cause additional problems.

NAILS

A Shar-pei's nails tend to grow fast and tough; it is wise, therefore, to start nail trimming at an early age. Dogs that have plenty of opportunity to exercise outdoors, and on rough surfaces, will be able to keep their nails short and trim; but those that stay mainly in the house or those kept on soft, grassy areas or soft ground will need frequent nail trims.

The longer the time a nail is left to grow, the more difficult it is to cut. A light-colored nail, seen in good light, will often disclose the pink blood vessel within, called the "quick." On a dark-colored nail, however, it is not apparent and extreme care should be exercised when trimming. Cutting into the quick is very painful and may result in future struggles with the dog whenever the need for a manicure arises.

Keep a container of styptic powder or a styptic pencil handy in case a nail does get clipped too short and bleeds. Plain flour may also be used in an emergency.

Holding your Shar-pei gently and carefully, snip off just the very tip of each nail. Don't frighten the dog by grabbing and hanging onto his legs for dear life (Shar-peis can put up quite a fight, and you will both be exhausted and miserable when it is over!) Don't forget to praise your dog and make a big fuss over him after you have finished the trimming of his nails.

DEWCLAWS

Many Shar-peis retain their dewclaws (extra claws or functionless digits on the inside of the leg), some even having double dewclaws. These should not be overlooked; unless checked from time to time, they will continue to grow and may circle back into the dog's leg, causing pain and infection. The double dewclaws, incidentally, are believed to have been handed down from the Tibetan Mastiff (a breed that may have played an important part in the origin of the Shar-pei).

Some breeders prefer to leave the dewclaws alone, believing the dogs should be shown in their natural state. Some purists feel that the original Shar-peis may have used their dewclaws in fighting, so these are worth preserving in the breed today. This may very well be true, considering the dewclaws tend to be long, sharp, and strong. If you feel that they should be removed—the breed standard suggests removing the hindleg dewclaws—this is best accomplished when the dog is just a few days old. Your veterinarian is the one to consult about the procedure.

I would like to mention here that while I was medicating one of my bitches, who wasn't cooperating, I received a nasty slash across my hand from one of her front dewclaws. It happened twice, in fact, and I'll never know whether it was done intentionally or accidentally.

FLEAS

Fleas must be kept off your Shar-pei, as a great many dogs are extremely allergic to them. In the case of allergic reaction, a single flea could have your pet scratching himself raw and bloody overnight.

Personally, I do not encourage the use of flea collars as a perpetual preventive, but there are many excellent sprays, powders, and dips that your veterinarian can recommend. Be sure to change the product periodically as fleas *do* build up a resistance to chemicals. If you have wondered why the flea product that used to work so well doesn't seem to be doing the job anymore, it is quite likely that the fleas in your area have built up a resistance to the product and it is time for a new one. A word of caution: some products are not compatible. Be sure to read the labels carefully and ask your vet for advice whenever you're in doubt. If you have a persistent flea problem, attention must also be given to the yard and home on a regular basis; in other words, both the dog *and* his environment need to be treated in order to eradicate these pests.

DEMODECTIC MANGE

Caused by the mite, *Demodex canis,* this condition is one with which the Shar-pei is plagued. It begins with small dry areas that may appear on the head, chest, and legs. As the dog scratches itself to relieve the intense itching, these areas become raw and red. Years ago dogs that developed the condition were put down; today, however, there are various products and medications which your vet can prescribe. But beware, as many products are toxic. Since the Shar-pei has sensitive skin (yes, even under that prickly coat), it makes sense to check with your veterinarian first before dipping your dog in some commercial preparation.

IMPACTED ANAL GLANDS

On each side and just below the dog's anus are sacs that contain small glands. These sacs secrete a brown, waxy substance that has a strong, putrid, long-lasting odor. The glands are much like those

Bedlam's Mortisha **(top),** bred by the author and owned by Jo Ann Webster of Fingertail Kennel. This black female, a six-month-old, is plagued with a staph infection and demodectic mange **(bottom).** Fortunately, your veterinarian can prescribe medicines and preparations that will keep these skin diseases under control.

Down-Homes Gretal of Eshaf **(top)** and Eshaf's Fat-Hui, a sable male with a short "horse" coat, **(bottom).** Both dogs owned by Emil and Vern Fahse of Eshaf's Kennels, Cicero, Illinois. Fat-Hui is by Wyloway Maistrivellen out of Eshaf's Li-Ming.

of a skunk—if the animal becomes frightened, the anal glands discharge their contents. Immediately, you detect an offensive odor.

The secretion may build up and form an impaction. Occasionally the glands will become infected; that is to say, an abscess will form, skin over the area will swell and redden, and the entire area will be extremely painful for the dog. You may notice your dog "scooting" his hindquarters across the floor or carpet in an effort to relieve the pressure of the impaction.

If your veterinarian is not available, and if there is no abscess present, locate the swollen glands by gently probing with your thumb and forefinger (you may want to first grasp a piece of tissue paper so as not to get the waxy discharge on yourself). The swollen glands should feel like two marbles. Gently squeeze with the thumb and forefinger until the contents of the glands have been extracted. If the substance is creamy in color, it is likely that infection has already set in; for this, you will need a good antibiotic ointment. Abscesses, however, should be treated by your veterinarian. If impacted anal glands become a chronic condition, the vet may recommend their removal.

RECTAL PROLAPSE

We thought it helpful to make some mention of rectal prolapse in the grooming section, for as you tend to your Shar-pei's ears, eyes, mouth, nails, and such, you should inspect other areas of the body as well to make sure everything is in good order. Characterized by a small or large red mass that is inflamed (even bloody) which protrudes from the anus, rectal prolapse often results from a dog's straining to defecate. Urinary obstruction, infection, prostate disease in males, and birth difficulties are also causes. A few cases in Shar-peis have been reported to date; however, we bring it to your attention because we may see more rectal prolapse in our breed now that the standard calls for more of a protruding anus. Veterinary care is in order for those individuals suffering from this disorder.

The preceding sections describe a few of the health problems that are seen in Shar-peis. It is recommended that you consult with a veterinarian as soon as you purchase your new prickly friend, since he or she can advise you on what other problems may arise and how best to deal with them.

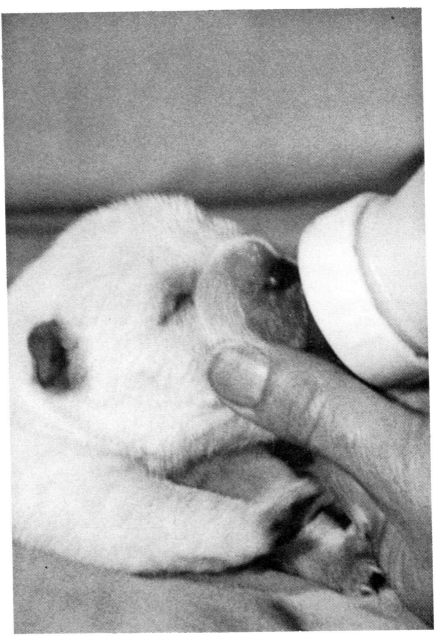

If for some reason you have to hand-feed a youngster, hold the sides of the pup's mouth closed around the bottle to allow better suction of milk and to eliminate the sucking in of air. Be sure to keep the head level.

Chapter 5

Feeding

Providing your dog with a nutritious diet throughout his life will supply him with a natural ability to fight off many diseases and live a long, healthy life. Proper nutrition is no longer a complicated task, as today's commercially available dog foods have been prepared to supply your dog with all of his basic food needs.

WHEN TO FEED

Although one generous meal a day will suffice, the most common feeding pattern among today's dog owners is to give a small meal or just a few dog biscuits in the morning and a big meal in the late afternoon or early evening. This system originated with the use of herding dogs. Since food tended to make the dog sluggish, he was fed after he finished his day's work. Owners of guard dogs, who work primarily at night, reverse the usual pattern and feed the dog his big meal in the morning—which is after work for the dog. This pattern should not be followed for growing puppies, who may need up to four meals a day. Most dogs grow in two years, the equivalent of what it takes humans twenty-five years, so maintain an adequate diet during this high growth period and decrease intake thereafter.

TYPES OF FOOD

Dogs have tolerant digestive systems that are well adapted to handling concentrated foods, such as meat. Their diet must be high in protein and have a sufficient amount of carbohydrates, fats, vitamins, and minerals. Clean, fresh water is an essential requirement and should be available at all times and changed daily.

Today's commercially prepared name-brand foods are the product of years of research into nutrition and are convenient and economical. These products are generally fortified with vitamins and minerals to supplement the natural value of the ingredients, which can suffer a substantial vitamin loss during processing.

There are three main types of prepared foods: dry, semimoist, and canned. The dry food is the most economical and generally requires only the addition of water (or it can be served "as is"). However, dry food may not contain enough fat, so you should add some meat scraps or broth to increase the nutritional value. One disadvantage—from the dog's point of view—is that dry food may be quite tasteless and it often becomes mushy when water is added, thereby sticking to the roof of the dog's mouth. The semimoist cereals or burgers have been judged more palatable, although generally there are more preservatives added to these products than to others. A small percentage of dogs react to these additives by scratching or biting at their skin, in which case the diet should be changed. Canned food is very popular with dogs and can be added to dry foods or cereals or served on its own. While it is the most expensive prepared food, it is not essential that the dog be fed canned food each day. Two or three servings a week should suffice. A diet of strictly canned food encourages the build-up of tartar on the dog's teeth, as there is no texture in the food to abrade the tooth surface. A diet combining several of the food types, aided by an occasional nylon chew bone (Nylabone®), will serve your dog well.

When selecting a particular brand of dog food, read the label for the product's contents and an analysis of its ingredients. The main ingredients are listed in order of content amount. The protein element should be among the first three ingredients. Do not buy a canned food that contains more than 75% water, as you are not getting much product for your money. Compare several brands before making your final selection, and be sure to choose one that is nutritionally complete and balanced as recommended by the National Research Council.

Some meats—canned or fresh—can be irritants to a dog's system. A small number of dogs have been found to be allergic to beef products that contain chemical additives to prevent spoilage. For some dogs, pork is hard to digest, while others experience diarrhea after eating liver. Be alert for signs of distress if you feed these meats to your dog. Older dogs often suffer from kidney problems and a heavy meat diet often overloads their systems with excess protein. Your veterinarian will generally prescribe modifications to the diet of older dogs to avoid health complications.

HOW MUCH IS ENOUGH?

A growing puppy should be plump, but as he grows he loses this "baby fat" and grows into a lean, firm adult. To determine if your dog is properly fed, run your hands over his ribs and hip bones. If these bones are very easily seen or felt, he may be underweight. If the bones are padded and hard to find, he may be overweight.

An overweight dog is the product of too much food and too little exercise. To help a dog regain his proper weight, cut back slightly on the amount of food you give and substitute low- calorie foods, such as raw green beans, low-fat cottage cheese, and cooked vegetables. These foods add bulk but not a lot of calories. Increase his physical activity, slowly at first, and maintain this higher level of exercise to keep off all lost weight and to tone the muscles.

All dogs will benefit from receiving nutritious table scraps with their meals. Most vegetables, cereals, and fruits are good additives, but do not give your dog any sweets or products with sugar, seasoned meats, or vegetables that produce gas (Brussels sprouts, cabbage, or broccoli).

At mealtime, allow the dog an adequate amount of time to finish his meal (twenty to thirty minutes). If any food remains in the feeding dish after this period, remove and discard it. If this pattern occurs several times, cut back on his rations until the dog finishes his meal in one visit to the dish. Serving more food than his hunger calls for encourages overeating and obesity, which can be life-threatening in dogs. As his activity levels change, you may have to increase or decrease the amount of food you give him to correspond to his needs. In the winter, if your dog spends a considerable amount of time outdoors, you should increase his daily rations by approximately 20% to help him maintain his body heat. Feed him additional fats and foods of high caloric content.

While most dogs will eat the same food every day without complaint, it is advisable to offer a slight variation every now and again. By serving a variety of foods you can avoid potential stomach or bowel troubles that can occur when his intake is forced to change due to your travel plans or to shortages of his usual food. Should you need to change your dog's diet from one main food to another, try to make the changeover as gradual as possible by first adding just a small amount of the new food to his regular meal. Increase the portion of new food daily—watching for signs of digestive distress—until he is accustomed to it.

PROBLEM EATERS

Should your dog be a "picky" eater, there are several methods that may help to stimulate his appetite. Give him only a half ration every once in a while to make him hungrier and more agreeable about eating what is given him. This does not mean that you should starve him, however. Chicken and liver are usually temptations that even a picky eater cannot refuse, as are small amounts of cheese. Do not give these as meals or between- meal snacks, as this may make him even more finicky. Adding a teaspoon of brewer's yeast (for every thirty pounds of body weight) to his meal is said to improve the appetite, but monitor the dog closely after use as this yeast has been associated with stomach bloating in some animals.

If your dog is a good eater and is still underweight, try switching to a different brand of food and supplementing his meals with meat scraps, cooked eggs, and cottage cheese. You may want to have your veterinarian check for the presence of worms or another disorder, should this augmented diet fail to put some weight on the dog. While a healthy dog may skip a meal now and then, if your dog should refuse his food for more than two days, consult your veterinarian.

The "gulper" is the opposite of the picky eater. He is so eager for his food that he takes large mouthfuls and quickly empties his bowl. Such a method of eating often results in a mess, as the dog's stomach cannot handle the sudden onslaught of food and the dog vomits the food back. A gulper is also taking in a lot of air with his food, which could encourage a life-threatening condition called

94

Shir Du Sam Ku with his owner, Ellen Weathers Debo **(top)**. Sam has a terrible attitude about cameras. He hates to be photographed and will flatten his ears, roach his back, and slink off at the slightest opportunity! Even as a four-month-old puppy, Sam projected a haughty attitude **(bottom)**.

95

bloat. To slow the gulper down, divide his daily rations into several small meals and give them to him at regular intervals. Monitor him. As his eating improves, increase the size of the meals until they are of normal proportion. Another method is to use a very large feeding dish and place a few large, inedible objects (such as nylon bones) in the bowl as obstacles to his eating. Having to maneuver around the objects will slow him down considerably. The gulper will usually grow out of the habit as he matures, as the gulping is often a habit he picked up as a young puppy when he felt it necessary to beat his littermates to the food source. Once he is assured that he will be able to get his fill, even if he dawdles a bit, he should settle into a normal eating pattern.

VITAMINS AND MINERALS

Many nutritionists claim that vitamin and mineral supplements can help pets live longer, healthier lives. While most commercially available foods for dogs have been enriched during preparation to include all the essential nutrients, there are certain situations where dogs may require additional doses of certain elements. One of the clearest cases is when an overweight dog is put on a restricted intake diet. As the amount of food the dog receives is reduced, so is the amount of vitamins and minerals that he is obtaining from his diet. You should consider giving a vitamin supplement to ensure proper nutrition if the dog is to remain on this low-calorie diet for an extended period of time.

Vitamin E has been shown to help improve a poor coat and help clear up minor skin irritations. Vitamin supplementation is commonly used to help bitches whelp faster and easier by replacing the elements that are divided from the mother to the puppies during pregnancy.

Some owners believe that brewer's yeast, which is rich in vitamin B-complex, is a natural flea repellent and a safer choice than chemical pesticides. Adding a little (one teaspoon per thirty pounds of body weight) of the yeast to the dog's food is said to produce a sulfurous taste on the dog's skin that the fleas don't like, so they leave him for a more suitable host. Others believe that frequent scratching or biting at the skin is a sign of vitamin deficiency which can be cleared up by supplementation.

Overleaf caption:
The eyes on this handsome five-week-old, "Bullet," are healing nicely. The sutures around his eyes are evidence that he has had corrective surgery for eye entropion. Owners, Jim and Karen Wang of Lexington, Kentucky.

Overleaf captions:
1. Three Sisters' Hera, Hannibal, and Halloweena at eight weeks. June Collins, breeder.
2. Sui-Yeen's Ta-Yang, bred by Rose Stone. **3.** J. P. Chan's Fei Tsai Kwun, a three-year-old male. This dog belongs to Cho Sun Kennel, Hong Kong. **4.** Hon. Ch. Jade East Hei Mi Te Otto by Hon. Ch. Gold's Chu Tein of Borden out of Reddy's Black Gem O'Bedlam. Loretta Anders, Greenville, South Carolina, owner. **5.** Half brothers Ch. Show Me Oogie's Fingertail, a one-year-old fawn male bred by Jackie Bulgin and owned by Don Wieden, and Show Me Bing's Fingertail, a one-and-a-half-year-old male also bred by Jackie and owned by Jo Ann Webster of Fingertail Kennel. Oogie was the first American Shar-pei champion imported to England. **6.** Boawnchein's Argie Fu Chew, bred by Bob and Dawn Walling of Sunol, California. **7.** An Argie Fu Chew—Attila Te Han offspring, Shar Jac's No-Spa of Boawnchein, pictured at ten weeks. Bred by the Wallings. **8.** Bedlam's Flirtation at three years, owned by the author.

1 ▶

2 ▶

3 ▶

4 ▶

5 ▶

6 ▶

7 ▶

8 ▶

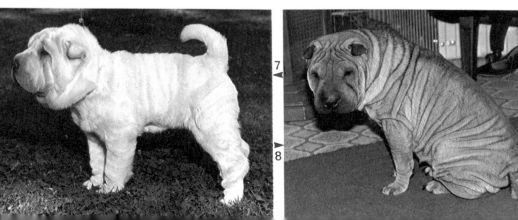

1▲   ▼2

1. A beautiful "flowered" or spotted puppy who, no doubt, will make an appealing pet. Chinese breeders believe the spotting indicates that other dog breeds were introduced into the line; this is why solid colors are preferred in Shar-peis. 2. Nice head study of a Bedlam Kennel's Shar-pei. 3. To simplify housebreaking, a puppy should be confined to a particular room. A large crate or a kennel could be used, or a room could be partitioned off. 4. ZL's Snuffle, known as "Snuffy," bred by Dick and Zell Llewellyn of Shoestring Acres, Alvin, Texas. 5. Ho Wun II Buddha sired these ten-week-old fawn males out of Bedlam's Mortisha. Breeder, Jo Ann Webster of Fingertail Kennel, Raritan, New Jersey. 6. ZL's Izzy "Best," bred by the Llewellyns.

1 ▶

2 ▶

3 ▶

4 ▶

5 ▶

6 ▶

106

1. Tsihmao's Hu-Tieh, out of Dah Let's Asha, bred by Linda Reinelt of Suderau, West Germany. **2.** Puppies from Bedlam Kennels. When you buy a Shar-pei pup from a reputable breeder, chances are you will be able to see the dog's parents and littermates. It is important to find out all you can about your prospective pet before making your purchase. **3.** Three-year-old Bedlam's Panda, C.D., bred by Ellen Weathers Debo and owned by Maryann Smithers of Oriental Treasure, Boonton, New Jersey. **4.** These pups are all littermates by the black stud Shir Du Sam Ku and the black bitch Bedlam's Black Storm. Their grandparents also were black. Breeder, Ellen Weathers Debo. **5.** Bedlam's Panda tends her youngsters. After a bitch has whelped, insist that she leave the nest to relieve herself. She will be reluctant to leave her new family, but this respite will be in her best interest. Offer her some food and something to drink, such as broth or water. **6.** Shar-peis get along well with other canine pets. "Chang," owned by Phyllis Lipisko of Scranton, Pennsylvania, and "Missy," a Yorkshire Terrier owned by the author, are the best of friends. **7.** Oriental Treasure's Impulse, a ten-week-old bred and owned by Maryann Smithers of Boonton, New Jersey. **8.** Bedlam's Beauty by Sis Q's Chin-Ho out of Ausables China Blue. Ellen Weathers Debo, breeder.

1▲ ▼2

Overleaf captions:
1. Ch. Gold's Taffy Apple Hau Jou bred by Gayle and the late Marty Gold, House of Gold, Charlotte, North Carolina. **2.** Chinese Shar-pei puppies present an appealing picture with wrinkles and rolls in abundance. As they mature, they grow into a large percentage of their coat, and it is not uncommon for a very wrinkled puppy to end up as a fairly tight-coated adult. These Fingertail pups were bred by Jo Ann Webster, Raritan, New Jersey.

110

Overleaf captions:
1. The author holds one of her puppies—a real bundle of love. As soon as you decide on a name for your Shar-pei pup, use it often so that the dog learns it quickly. **2.** Bedlam's Flirtation looking as glamourous as ever! Bred by the author. **3.** It's no wonder people are intrigued with our breed; just look at that face. Fingertail Bumble was bred by Jo Ann Webster of Fingertail Kennel, Raritan, New Jersey. **4.** The very noble Oriental Treasure's All That Jazz at four months. Bred and owned by Maryann Smithers of Boonton, New Jersey.

111

114

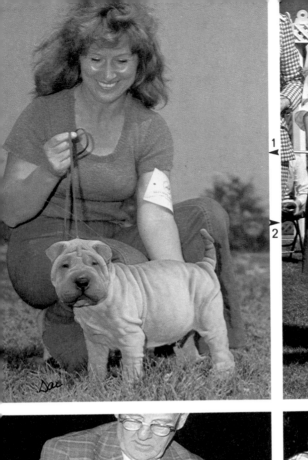

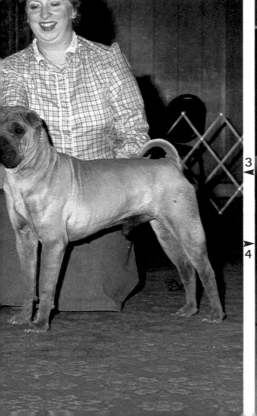

1. Best of Winners goes to Ch. Gold's Teak of Chu Tien, handled by Dawn Walling, at a 1982 Oriental Breeds International match show. **2.** Unfortunately a solid pink tongue is now considered a fault in Shar-peis. Here three-month-old Bedlam's Yo Ki Hi is owner/handled by the author. **3.** Jo Ann Gremminger of House of Tzo Tzo wins Best of Opposite Sex with one of her dogs at the Greater Midwest Chinese Shar-pei Fanciers' Dog Show, 1983. The judge was Joan Urban. **4.** Hon. Ch. Go-Lo's Ark Kee winning first place at a 1984 fun match (City of Fairfax Chamber of Commerce). Jo Ann and Duncan Redditt of Alexandria, Virginia, owners.

119

GREATER MISSISSIPPI
VALLEY CHINESE
SHAR-PEI CLUB

BEST
PUPPY

OCT. 16, 1983

JUDGE H. COMPTON

Overleaf captions:
1. Ch. Alpha Chanel Moshu at six months going Best of Opposite Sex for Pamela Hurley of Alpha Reg. Kennel, Monclova, Ohio. By Ch. Shangri-la's Gogorila Teabaggy out of Hurley's Shen Te Mi. **2.** Bright Willow of Hau Jou, breeder/handled by Pat Goodale, winning Best Puppy under judge H. Compton. Owners, John and Betsy Davison, Loong Ch'ai Kennel, Sarasota, Florida. **3.** Down-Homes Milky W Star II, sister to Down-Homes Cream Woo, pictured at three months. Breeder, Matgo Law of Hong Kong. **4.** Two-year-old Ch. Sterling's Rinky Ding finishing his championship. Owned by Maryann Smithers of Oriental Treasure, Boonton, New Jersey. **5.** Oriental Treasure's X-tra Trouble, bred and owned by Maryann Smithers. **6.** Steve Nash handles Ausables China Blue to Best Puppy in Non-Sporting Group, May 1975. Ellen Weathers Debo, owner.

122

Overleaf captions:
1. Best of Opposite Sex is awarded to one-and-a-half-year-old Ch. Oriental Treasure's Honey, bred and owned by Maryann Smithers of Boonton, New Jersey. **2.** If you are thinking seriously about showing your Shar-pei, you can either show the dog yourself or seek the services of a professional handler. Photo courtesy of Maryann Smithers. **3.** Boawnchein's Sesame O'Kenlane, a ten-week-old by Ho-Ti Mucho Macho Man of Foo out of Boawnchein's Ty-P-Bits of Eshaf. Breeder-owner-handled by Dawn Walling of Boawnchein Kennels, Sunol, California. **4.** Best in Match Junior Puppy awarded to Oriental Treasure's X-tra Trouble, a three-month-old, breeder-owner-handled by Maryann Smithers.

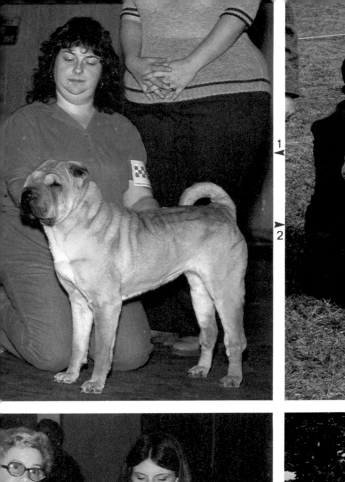

1

2

3

4

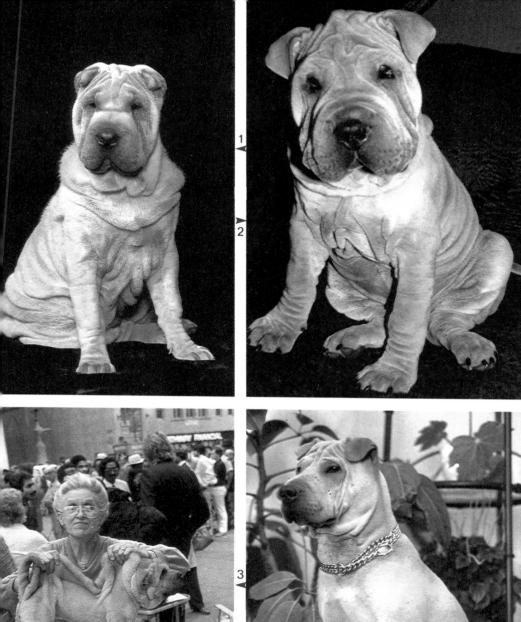

126

Infirm older dogs have reportedly been aided by receiving daily doses of vitamins C and B-complex. These vitamins are said to help alleviate joint discomfort and allow the dog to move more freely. On a similar note, there is a claim (as yet unconfirmed) that high doses of vitamin C can help stop hip dysplasia, a crippling genetic hip disorder commonly found in the larger breeds. Some breeders believe that supplementing a pregnant bitch's diet with vitamin C will aid in producing puppies that are less prone to hip dysplasia. Others believe that high doses of this vitamin should be given to puppies during their high- growth periods to help prevent the disease and that high doses of vitamin C will keep the disease from progressing in dogs already exhibiting signs of this abnormality. It must be stressed that these claims are still under investigation and currently very controversial.

CHEWING

Throughout the dog's life there is a strong need for him to chew. As a puppy, chewing assists in cutting the puppy teeth and assuring normal jaw development. As he grows, the dog must chew to help rid himself of the baby teeth and make way for the permanent teeth, which appear at four to seven months. This teething process continues for more than a year as the teeth and jaw bones develop.

Without proper chewing diversions, a young dog can be very destructive, often destroying hundreds of dollars worth of household items. Shoes and items made of leather are favorite selections, as well as the more dangerous electric cords, which can cause injury and death.

Even as the dog matures past this critical period of development, the need to chew remains. Chewing on abrasive surfaces is the only way a dog knows to rid his teeth of the irritating tartar or plaque that accumulates at his gum line. Left unchecked, such tartar will erode the enamel of the teeth and eventually destroy the teeth at the roots.

Emotional factors such as loneliness, fear, or boredom bring on bouts of destructive chewing. Left confined or alone for long stretches of time, dogs often find relief in chewing their tensions away.

Since it is inevitable and, in fact, beneficial for dogs to chew, conscientious owners must supply their pets with a nondestructive

Sisters, one eleven-and-a-half months and the other three-and-a-half-months old, at play **(top).** Eshaf's Ju-Lo-Yen-Se, a true cream bitch with a brick-colored nose, by Down-Homes Man-Poon out of Eshaf's Quein-Yen **(bottom).** All dogs bred by Emil and Vern Fahse of Eshaf's Kennels, Cicero, Illinois.

outlet for these chewing energies. The main point to remember is that the dog must not be allowed to chew an item that is potentially dangerous to him. It must appeal to his chewing instincts, yet be safe and durable. Dogs should never be allowed to chew on an object that can break into sizeable chunks, which when swallowed can pierce the walls of the stomach or intestines. Indigestible items, such as rubber toys or cheap plastic bones, can become lodged in the dog's intestines if swallowed, requiring emergency surgery to remove this blockage before it leads to a painful death.

The chewing of bones can be a useful means of tooth cleaning for the dog, but you should avoid giving your dog bones that splinter— especially those from chicken, turkey, and fish. While most animal bones are flexible when raw, after cooking they become brittle and can cause damage to the dog's mouth and digestive tract. Beef shin or marrow bones, in approximately six- inch lengths, are very sturdy and popular with dogs whose mouths are large enough to accommodate them. Such bones are, however, highly abrasive. If your dog chews excessively, the use of such bones may cause his teeth to become dangerously worn down in a few years' time, leaving them in a painful, irreparable condition.

Rawhide products are quite popular, but they do not fulfill the dog's chewing requirements very well. Once given to the dog, they quickly become very messy as the rawhide gets wet from mouthing. Most dogs are able to quickly chew them up, making them uneconomical. Additionally, research in the last few years has shown that rawhide pieces can become lodged in a dog's throat and these have been responsible for a number of deaths. The rawhide chunks mix with the saliva in the throat and swell, cutting off the air supply and causing the dog to asphyxiate. Undigested pieces of rawhide have also been associated with cases of severe constipation, as they can cause intestinal blockage.

Nylon bones are generally considered the most economical and safe chew items for dogs. While they are quite sturdy and long-lasting, they are at the same time unabrasive to the surface of the dog's teeth. Hard chewing causes the surface to give off bristle-like shavings that effectively clean the tooth surface and massage the gum line. When swallowed by the dog, these shavings are broken down by the dog's digestive juices and they pass harmlessly through the dog's system. Because of the toughness of the nylon,

There is nothing like a good Nylabone®, whether you have it all to yourself **(top, left)** as "Barney" has, or whether you share it with a friend **(top, right)** the way Shir Du Sam Ku and Bedlam's Yo Ki Hi have. Nylabones **(bottom)** are the safest chew toys to give your dog, as they will not splinter or chip.

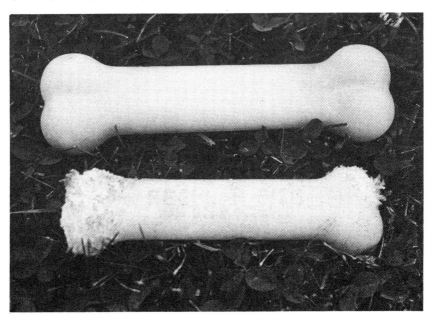

132

dogs cannot break off large chunks of the bone, which makes them safe alternatives to animal bones. Nylon is also more sanitary than other material used to make bones, as it does not support the growth of micro-organisms and can be easily cleaned with soap and water.

Nylabone® is highly recommended by veterinarians as a safe, healthy nylon bone that cannot splinter or chip. Instead, Nylabone® is frizzled by the dog's chewing action, creating a tooth-brush-like surface that cleanses the teeth and massages the gums. Nylabone®, Nylaball®, and Nylaring®, the only chew products made of flavor-impregnated solid nylon, are available in local pet shops everywhere.

As a dog requires the use of his teeth throughout his life, owners should routinely inspect the condition of the dog's mouth. While vigorous chewing should keep tartar build-up to a minimum, most dogs will require a professional tooth scraping at least once or twice in their adult life. Be alert to any changes in your dog's eating or chewing behavior for signs of possible distress.

Bedlam's Peachy Keen, owned by the author. By Shir Du Sam Ku (Albright Ho Hsiung x Walnut Lanes Chiu Chei Chu) out of Bedlam's Stormy (Shir Du Sam Ku x Down-Homes Oriental Pearl).

Down-Homes Cream Zulu, World champion, German and Luxembourg champion, and winner of various other titles. Owner, Joachim Weinberg, Hamburg, West Germany.

134

Chapter 6

General Husbandry

A nutritious diet and adequate exercise are necessary requirements for keeping a dog in good physical condition. The most obvious sign that your dog is not getting enough exercise is excess weight, but there are other indications. If your dog is overactive or restless in the house, he may need more time outside for vigorous activity. Pets with excess energy may show signs of anxiety or become destructive in the house. A dog in good physical condition is better able to withstand disease, remain mentally alert, and live a longer life.

To test your dog's physical trim, feel his muscles in the shoulder and thighs. They should be firm and not soft and flabby. A doopy undercarriage is also evidence that more exercise is needed.

All dogs kept as housepets need to be taken out regularly, at least three times a day to relieve themselves and be exposed to some fresh air. In addition, most dogs will benefit from at least twenty minutes of vigorous exercise. If you live in the city, daily workouts may necessarily be limited to walks and an occasional run in the park. Country dogs, on the other hand, have greater opportunities for exercise. Swimming is an excellent activity that works all the muscles, and most dogs love it. Another favorite exercise—one that is easy on the dog owner—is to have the animal chase and retrieve a ball or stick. This game can be played not only outdoors, but indoors as well, which can be very useful during periods of inclement weather. If you have access to a large

135

amount of open land, try tossing a frisbee for your dog to retrieve. This is an excellent overall exercise and most dogs love the chasing and leaping that are involved. *Warning:* golf balls do not make suitable toys. They are made under great pressure and have been known to explode upon hard contact.

If your dog has a sedentary life and you wish to help him get back in shape, increase his activity level very slowly to avoid overexertion or strained muscles. This is especially important for older dogs. They still need exercise, but in moderate amounts. One extra walk a day will quickly build a dog's stamina.

In times of extreme weather, take precautions when exposing the dog to the elements. In the heat of summer, curtail all vigorous activity during the hottest times of the day and exercise the dog only in the cool of the late evening or early morning. Be sure to have plenty of fresh water available at all times to help prevent heatstroke. In the winter, dogs that are normally confined to the warmth of the house can be very sensitive to great drops in temperature. To avoid a chill and possible illness, supply the dog with a sweater during very cold periods and always be sure to thoroughly dry him once he has come back into the house. This is especially important for older or infirm dogs who can quickly succumb to illness.

When walking the dog at night, a piece of reflective tape on his collar will help make him more visible to motorists.

DOG HOUSES

If your dog is to spend a considerable amount of time outdoors, he will need to have protection from the elements. He will need a place to find shade in the summer and shelter in the winter. If possible, he should be supplied with cover that is well insulated, one that is warm in cold weather and stays cool in the heat of the summer.

For one dog, a dog house would seem the logical choice. It should not be so heavy as to be immovable and it must be placed on ground that drains well. The bottom of the house should never be placed directly on the ground so that it can quickly rot but should be slightly elevated to help keep dampness to a minimum. This can be done by placing two or three bricks under each corner of the house or by building legs that extend six or eight inches from the bottom. The dog house should be painted white, as this helps to repel some of the sun's rays and keeps the temperature lowered inside during the summertime.

Whether you build your own dog house or purchase a ready-made version, there are several important features to keep in mind. The house should be constructed of weatherproof materials, with shingles or siding nailed onto the roof to help supply insulation. You should try to draft-proof the house. One way is to nail pieces of carpet or canvas to the door frame; these act as a curtain against the wind. Two pieces that overlap down the center work best to stop the wind from penetrating. A more effective method of preventing drafts is to partition the house into two separate compartments: a large sleeping chamber and an entrance hall. The door should be rather small—yet large enough to allow the dog to enter comfortably—and placed at the extreme left or right along one of the long sides of the dog house. By inserting a wall about half the width of the house to line the entranceway, the inner compartment is kept protected from the elements. A sill two or three inches high at the foot of the doorway also helps reduce drafts and keeps snow out in the winter. Regardless of dog-house style, it is advisable that a section of the roof or one of the sides be hinged for ease in cleaning and changing the bedding.

Bedding is an important part of the dog house. It supplies both warmth and comfort and helps protect your dog from getting sores and callouses on his elbows and hocks. The dog house should be routinely disinfected and the bedding changed frequently, as soiled bedding will attract such annoying pests as fleas, ticks, and lice. In the summer, four to five inches of straw, wood shavings, or shredded newspaper work best. In the winter you can add a blanket or an old mattress pad for more warmth; since these items absorb moisture easily, they must be checked daily for dampness.

PROTECTION FROM THEFT OR STRAYING

As the owner of a purebred dog, you recognize the beauty and quality of your pet. Most likely, he is viewed not only as a pet but as a member of your family. You should be aware that each year thousands of dogs are stolen, often because their owners let the dogs roam or left them unattended. The most common theft pattern occurs when dog owners tie their charges outside of a building or store while they "run a quick errand." Upon returning, their beloved pet is gone. Such a loss could be prevented with a few common sense actions. First and foremost, if you are going someplace where the dog cannot be allowed inside with you, *leave the dog at home*. Second, never allow your dog to run free without direct supervision. Regardless of how well trained he is, he can be lured away. Third, prepare for a potential loss by seeing to it that the dog can be properly identified.

In recent years tattooing has become a very popular method of ensuring that your dog could be identified if he were to become lost or stolen. Tattooing is a relatively painless procedure that can be performed by most veterinarians for a modest fee. If done properly, there is very little risk of infection and the tattooing can be done in several minutes' time.

Tattooing is usually performed on the groin area or inside the ear, although the groin is preferable since there have been reports of dogs having their ears cut off to rid the dog of his identification. Two types of numbers are generally used: the owner's social security number or the dog's AKC registration number. In the case of purebreds, the registration number is most often used to eliminate problems should the dog change owners during his lifetime. Several national registries exist that will record, for an annual fee, the dog's tattoo number and the name, address, and telephone number of his owner. Such registries have led to the safe return of many lost and stolen dogs. Your local kennel club should be able to supply you with the name and address of a registry in your area.

It is best to wait until your puppy reaches at least four months of age before having him tattooed, as you do not want to risk having the tattoo ink smear as the puppy grows and his skin stretches. For owners considering a show career for their dog, there is no reason to forego tattooing. The American Kennel Club has ruled that a tattoo is acceptable in show competition and cannot be penalized.

TRAVELING AND MOTION SICKNESS

One of the greatest pleasures of owning a well-trained dog is being able to enjoy his company wherever you go. If you wish your dog to be a traveling companion, start him off while he is still a puppy. Take him on short trips around town as well as on long drives. Through such exposure, traveling in the car will become routine and great fun.

The first few trips in the car should be short ones, and you should crate the dog for safety. It is advisable to have another passenger along with the driver to comfort the dog should he become frightened. Be prepared for an emergency clean-up, as young pups often relieve themselves out of fright or vomit in reaction to the unfamiliar motion. Drooling is a sign that the dog is not feeling well, so watch him carefully and let him out of the car at the first hint of sickness. Hopefully this will pass as the dog matures and learns how to relax while riding in the car. If your dog is prone to messes, you may want to line the crate with a towel or some newspapers to aid in the inevitable clean-up. Repetition is the best method for accustoming the dog to the car; do this by gradually lengthening the trips as the dog begins to adjust.

Most dogs take easily to traveling by car, but some are always physically upset by the motion. If this is the case with your dog and he does not outgrow this tendency toward motion sickness, consult your veterinarian about possible remedies.

For trips longer than just around town, there are several steps that may help your dog feel more comfortable during his confinement in the car. To help prevent nausea, never feed your dog a meal before traveling. Wait several hours after he has eaten before leaving on an extended trip. It is recommended that you take the dog for a brisk walk before leaving, both to give him a chance to relieve himself and to tire him a bit. He is more likely to settle in and take a nap while riding if he has been given an opportunity to release some energy before starting the trip. You should give him a drink of water *after* the drive, as the excitement of the trip will make him quite thirsty. If the trip is longer than one hour, plan on stopping halfway to give him a small drink and a chance to relieve himself.

AIR TRAVEL

In recent years traveling in an airplane has become much safer for animals, as stricter rules have been imposed on the airlines to insure the safety of their cargo. You should, however, investigate the safety record of the airlines you are considering, as some companies are more experienced and accommodating than others.

Try to arrange for as short a flight as possible, with a straight-through flight being preferable if at all possible. Be sure the dog's crate, as well as the dog himself, is properly identified. If you are not traveling with the dog, be sure to have a reliable source meeting the dog upon arrival at his new location. Give this person the name of the airline, the number of the flight, and the departure and arrival times. Make sure that this person agrees to contact you as soon as the dog arrives, as dogs have been known to get lost in flight and time is of the essence in locating a misdirected dog crate.

Crates can be purchased from pet shops or they are often available for rent from the airlines. The crate must be sturdy and only large enough to let the dog stand and change positions. If too large, the dog could be easily jostled and possibly injured. On the outside of the crate, plainly write the dog's destination, as well as your name and address. If there are any special instructions (such as possible medical problems), attach these to the outside of the crate where they can be easily read. If it is to be a long flight, you must also include feeding and exercise instructions. A health certificate should be obtained from your veterinarian and included with the dog to prove he has had his rabies and distemper inoculations, as some states will require this before the dog is released.

To make the trip as stress-free as possible, do not feed the dog for four or five hours before the flight. He must be exercised and allowed to relieve himself directly before and after the flight. Include a small amount of dry food in an attached container inside the crate and make sure there is an empty water dish attached to the inside of the crate also. It should be located on or near the door so that it can be filled by the airline personnel with little difficulty. Make the crate familiar to your dog by placing a favorite toy and his usual blanket inside.

If the dog appears overly nervous in his crate, you may wish to give him a mild tranquilizer before the flight. Consult your veterinarian for his advice on travel procedures and sedating animals before a flight.

BOARDING YOUR DOG

Situations occasionally arise when you must be separated from your dog for an extended period of time. If you are planning a vacation or trip in which your dog cannot be included, plan in advance for his care while you are away.

140

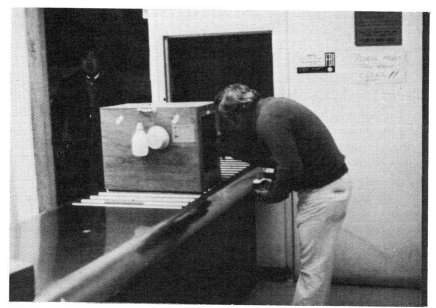

This Down-Homes puppy has travelled all the way from Hong Kong to his new home with the author in the United States. Before an imported dog is allowed to enter the country, it must pass through customs **(top)** and undergo medical inspection **(bottom)**.

Whatever method you select, put the dog's welfare first. The least traumatic solution would be to leave the dog at home, in his familiar surroundings, and hire a friend or neighbor to care for him. He should not be given free run of the house while unattended, but left confined to a suitable area. The dog will have to be walked and fed several times a day, and, hopefully, the person you select will give him some companionship and attention to keep him from becoming lonely (which can lead to destructiveness). Make sure the person you choose is reliable, and phone him a day or two into your trip to make sure that all is going well. This method is highly stressed for dogs that tend to be high strung, aggressive with strangers, or excessive barkers.

If you are planning to board the dog at a kennel, do some research before making your selection. Ask a friend, your veterinarian, or a pet shop proprieter for recommendations. Before dropping the dog off, visit the kennel to inspect it for cleanliness and to evaluate the care being given the dogs boarded there already and their current state of health. Also be aware of the kennel's security, as you do not want your dog to be able to escape or perhaps be stolen due to inadequate protection.

All boarding kennels require that the dogs shall have had all necessary immunizations prior to being accepted for boarding. This is to avoid outbreaks of communicable diseases. Upon arrival, inform the proprietor of your dog's medical history and, if he has a medical problem, be sure to leave the appropriate medicine and instructions on how to handle the condition.

Always leave with your dog's caretaker a telephone number where you can be reached, as well as the telephone number of the dog's veterinarian. Try to make the dog feel as much at home as possible before you leave him. Give him his favorite toy or blanket (if this is acceptable to the kennel), as this may help him adjust to the new surroundings.

CARE OF THE OLDER DOG

One of the keys to helping your dog live a long, healthy life is to watch his diet and weight from the time he is a puppy. Do not let him get overweight, as this puts excess strain on the heart and can result in a premature death. Exercise is a necessary requirement throughout his life, but as he ages most vigorous activities should be eliminated to prevent him from overexerting himself. This is especially important in hot weather. Substitute leisurely walks for energetic runs. As the older dog exercises less, his caloric intake should be cut down. Modify his diet as necessary, usually by cutting back his intake by ten to twenty percent.

Painful, arthritic joints are common in the older dog. You can help comfort him by supplying a comfortable bed for him to rest in—perhaps even a waterbed—and try to discourage him from climbing many stairs. Vitamin and mineral supplements have been acclaimed as aids in alleviating joint discomfort. Your veterinarian can advise which vitamins might be useful; perhaps he or she may prescribe medicines that restrict swelling in the joints and relieve pain. Exercise of any kind may be painful, but the arthritic dog must still be encouraged to move about or else the legs will get stiffer and more hurtful, eventually becoming useless. Exercise should, of course, be very moderate. It may also be comforting if you massage the dog's legs once or twice a day to stimulate blood flow and relieve tightness.

The teeth can be a major problem for older dogs. You should regularly check for tartar and remove all build-up. An abscessed tooth is a common malady that often goes undetected until visible signs, such as a purulent wound on the cheek or a loss of appetite, appear. Inspect your dog's mouth and have all diseased teeth removed as soon as they are detected, as infection can result from neglected dental problems.

Nap periods for canine senior citizens may become more frequent and longer, but be alert for signs of continual grogginess. This could be a sign of serious health problems, such as failing kidneys or an overtaxing of the digestive system. A slight increase in his intake of water is to be expected, but drinking excessive amounts of water may be a warning signal of distress. If there is any noticeable change in the dog's behavior, quickly consult your veterinarian or schedule an office visit.

As a dog ages, his eyesight and hearing may become less acute. With this comes an increased chance that the dog may not be able to swiftly respond or react to dangerous situations. Such impaired older dogs must not be allowed free access to the great outdoors. They should be taken out on leash and be more closely monitored than when they were young.

143

Boawnchein's Peko T, by Boawnchein's Argie Fu Chew out of Boawnchein's Attila Te Han, owned by Bob and Dawn Walling of Sunol, California **(top).** ZL's Mc Tavish **(bottom),** owned by Dick and Zell Llewellyn of Alvin, Texas.

144

Hearing problems can often be the result of ear mites or an accumulation of excess wax in the ear canal. Left unchecked such conditions can lead to a permanent loss of hearing. However, a thorough cleaning and the administration of some ear medication by a veterinarian can often clear up many hearing disorders in the older dog.

Make life as easy as possible for the infirm older dog by adapting to his needs. Do not change his daily routine, including such minor things as moving his water and food bowls to a new location, unless this is absolutely necessary. Talk to and pet an older dog often to reassure and comfort him.

As the older dog exercises less, his nails get less exposure to the rough surfaces that wear them down. Inspect the nails regularly and trim them when needed. The older dog also needs special care when exposed to the extremes of weather. His coat thins as he ages, so he should be covered with a coat or sweater in cold weather and kept dry to avoid sudden chills. In very hot weather keep him inside as much as possible to avoid heatstroke and dehydration, and provide lots of fresh water. If he appears to be suffering from the heat, a sponge bath with cool water will usually restore his normal body temperature.

Bedlam Kennels' Down-Homes Mr. Universe, owned by Ellen Weathers Debo. When selecting a Shar-pei puppy, always choose one that is the picture of good health: one that is active, bright-eyed, curious about its surroundings, and sturdy on its feet.

Chapter 7

Health Care

While there are literally thousands of diseases and problems that your dog *can* be subjected to during his lifetime, you should realize that he will most likely live a relatively healthy life. Given the proper blend of exercise, good nutrition, suitable housing, and routine veterinary care, your dog can be expected to be an active member of your household for many years. When it comes to health care, the main point to remember is that you are responsible for noticing any changes in your pet's behavior that may indicate a health problem, but the diagnosis and treatment should be left to a professional—your veterinarian. From the time you first bring the dog into your household, you should establish a regular pattern of veterinary visits. In this way your veterinarian gets the chance to become familiar with you and your dog, and the dog receives his necessary inoculations and examinations.

SUPPLIES

To be prepared for coping with a medical emergency, you should have within easy reach the following items:

- rectal thermometer
- petroleum jelly
- boric acid eyewash
- gauze or cotton bandages

- hydrogen peroxide or iodine
- cotton swabs
- tweezers
- blunt-tipped scissors
- bicarbonate of soda or mineral oil

These supplies can be used as aids in determining the extent of your dog's illness or to handle such minor injuries as cuts, bee stings, or small burns. With minor problems such as these, treat the ailment as you would that of a human. Keep all wounds clean to avoid infection and secure the advice of a veterinarian should there be any signs of complications in healing.

SIGNS OF ILLNESS

Should you notice that your dog is not acting normally, perhaps appearing overly tired and sluggish, review his vital signs. Take his temperature by using a rectal thermometer. Listlessness is often a sign of fever. Most major ailments cause a rise in temperature above the normal 101° to 102° range. A reading of two degrees above or below the normal is cause for concern and you should consult your veterinarian. A dog's normal pulse rate is from 80 to 140 beats per minute. The pulse is taken from a spot where the artery is near the surface, such as inside the hind leg where the leg meets the body. A very fast pulse can indicate shock, and a weak pulse can indicate a life-threatening condition. A final measure that is easily taken is respiration; a normal rate is from 10 to 30 breaths per minute.

A sudden loss of appetite can be a sign of various ailments: fever, a sore mouth, diseased teeth, or an upset stomach. If it should continue for more than twenty-four hours, a trip to the veterinarian is in order. Likewise with persistent vomiting or diarrhea. While most upsets pass quickly, do not delay in seeking help should your dog pass bloody urine or stools or appear to suffer a seizure.

INFECTIOUS DISEASES

Most communicable diseases that dogs are susceptible to can be prevented by obtaining the necessary series of vaccinations during your puppy's initial visits to the veterinarian. During the first

148

weeks of the puppy's life, he receives antibodies from his mother that protect him from disease. Once he is fully weaned, this natural protection is gone and the puppy is vulnerable until he is immunized. Until protected, it is important to keep puppies-at-risk in clean surroundings and limit their contact with other dogs and people who may be carriers of infectious diseases.

The first shots a puppy receives are weak doses that protect for only a short time, so it is vital that two follow-up shots also be administered. Generally a booster will be needed at one year, with yearly shots thereafter. Your veterinarian can set up an immunization schedule for your dog, so discuss this with him as soon as you bring your canine friend into your home. Prevention is the key, as these contagious diseases can be virtually eliminated if proper vaccination procedures are followed throughout your dog's life.

Rabies. This highly contagious viral disease is spread among warm-blooded animals through contact with infectious saliva, and transmission usually occurs by means of an infected animal's bite. The virus travels from the wound site through the central nervous system to the brain where it causes damage and noticeable behavioral changes. Dogs that have not been vaccinated against this dread disease are susceptible, so this is why preventive measures must be taken to ensure your pet is protected. Once a dog is bitten by a rabid animals and clinical signs appear, death soon follows.

The symptoms of rabies generally fall into two classifications. The first is "furious rabies," which begins with a period of depression or melancholy, followed by irritability. In the latter state the dog is most dangerous, as he may be prone to attack other animals or people. These first stages can last several hours to several days. During this time the dog will show little or no interest in eating, change his body position often, lick himself, and try to bite or swallow foreign objects. He becomes spasmodically wild and tries to bite everything around him. If caught and caged at this point, he will relentlessly try to free himself by attacking and biting at the bars that confine him, actions which often result in broken teeth and a fractured jaw. The rabid dog's bark becomes a peculiar howl. The final phase of the disease is marked by a paralysis of the dog's lower jaw which causes it to hang down. Hydrophobia sets in, since the animal is incapable of ingesting water. The dog walks with a stagger, saliva drips from his mouth, and he usually dies within four to eight days after the onset of paralysis.

The second classification of rabies is referred to as "dumb rabies," characterized by the dog's walking in a manner similar to that of a lumbering bear. The head is held down and the jaw is paralyzed. The dog is unable to bite, and he appears to have something caught in the back of his throat.

The only method of prevention is with the appropriate vaccine administered by a veterinarian. Keep in mind that a rabid dog is highly dangerous to humans and other animals; therefore, local public health officials should be contacted even if rabies is suspected. Dogs normally receive their first rabies shot at one year, but it may be administered earlier if the disease is prevalent in a particular municipality. A rabies booster shot, given once every two years, will protect your dog from this deadly disease.

Distemper. Puppies are most prone to contract distemper, which affects the lungs, intestines, and nervous system. It is a deadly disease, but it can be controlled by early inoculation with yearly booster shots reinforcing the protection. Symptoms of the disease are often subtle: loss of appetite and energy, fever and chills, and a discharge from the nose and eyes. If left untreated, the disease quickly intensifies and attacks many major body organs, leaving the dog susceptible to convulsions, paralysis, and death.

Although distemper usually attacks young puppies, dogs of any age can succumb. It is vital that you immunize all young dogs by taking them to the veterinarian at a very early age to protect them when they are most vulnerable, but annual boosters must also be maintained to continue the protection throughout the dog's life.

Leptospirosis. Another disease that can be prevented through proper immunization at an early age is leptospirosis. This disease is caused by rapidly growing bacteria that infect sewage or slow-moving or stagnant water pools. It can be carried by mice or rodents and is most often transmitted when a dog licks substances or objects that have been contaminated by the feces or urine of infected animals.

Symptoms of leptospirosis infection vary and may include: chronic diarrhea; vomiting; fever; depression; a dry coat; and a yellow discoloration of the teeth, tongue, and jaws, which is caused by an acute inflammation of the kidneys. Left unchecked, this disease is deadly, but it is easily controlled through administration of a vaccine (often in conjunction with distemper and hepatitis shots).

Hepatitis. This viral disease is one of the few infectious diseases that has increased in incidence in recent years. Hepatitis is easily spread through casual contact, and young dogs are the most susceptible. Like distemper, the primary symptoms are often subtle: loss of appetite and energy, vomiting, thirst, and fever. Swelling of the abdomen, head, and neck regions is also common. The disease increases in virulence very quickly, and veterinary care is essential as death can occur in just a few hours. Hepatitis can, however be prevented by a vaccination.

Parainfluenza. This contagious respiratory disease, commonly referred to as *kennel cough,* often attacks whole litters of puppies; in fact, it can devastate entire kennels of dogs. Caused by a virus, the most obvious symptom of this disease is coughing, and a general decline in physical condition follows. An afflicted dog is left very weak and susceptible to other debilitating diseases.

Parainfluenza outbreaks spread very quickly, so it is essential to have all dogs immunized against this deadly disease.

Canine Parvovirus. (CPV). This viral disease is not only highly contagious and deadly, but it is often hard to get rid of once an area becomes exposed. The virus is spread chiefly through the feces of infected dogs, and it is capable of existing in the host environment for months at a time. Major disinfection techniques must be applied to rid an afflicted area of the virus.

The incidence of canine parvovirus has been on the increase in recent years, so prevention by means of a vaccination is essential. CPV attacks the intestinal tract, the white blood cells, and often the heart muscle. The symptoms are vomiting, diarrhea or blood-streaked feces, fever, loss of appetite and energy, and dehydration. These symptoms generally appear five to seven days after exposure to the virus. Puppies are the primary victims, as it often proves fatal to young dogs, but older dogs seem to be able to combat the disease more efficiently.

As with most infectious diseases, the best preventative is immunization by the administration of a vaccine by your veterinarian. If you maintain any type of kennel or outdoor housing, it is advisable to disinfect the area routinely as a precautionary measure.

One part household bleach to thirty parts water can be used effectively. Whenever you take your dog for a walk, do not let him come into contact with the feces of other dogs, as this may be a source of CPV infection.

INTERNAL PARASITES

It is very common for dogs, especially when young, to become infected with internal parasites (worms). While most infestations are not severe and are easily cured by medication, if left unchecked worms can cause permanent damage and death. During your puppy's first checkup your veterinarian will look for the presence of worms by examining a stool sample under a microscope. This is the only way to determine exactly which type of parasite, if any, is present and to prescribe the correct treatment.

As your dog ages you should have routine tests for worms performed when he receives his yearly shots. In the time between veterinary visits, be on the lookout for evidence of internal parasites, such as small worms clinging to the dog's bedding, feces, or hair around the anus. He may also "scoot" or drag his backside across the floor (although scooting can also be a sign of overfilled or infected anal glands). If worms are suspected, have your veterinarian perform the necessary diagnostic tests to identify the infestation. *Do not* worm the dog yourself with over-the- counter preparations unless so advised by your veterinarian. This is a common source of accidental poisonings, as dosages in excess of what is recommended are often administered by well-meaning owners.

There are several preventive measures that can be taken to lessen the chances of your dog's becoming infested with internal parasites. A healthy, well-nourished dog is more apt to remain worm-free because of his high stamina than a weak dog. Provide a diet that is high in protein and rich in vitamin A. Proper sanitation is a must. Be sure that the dog's bedding is kept clean and dry to avoid its becoming infested with fleas, ticks, and other external parasites, which are often the carriers of internal parasites.

There are five common types of worms seen in dogs: roundworms, tapeworms, hookworms, whipworms, and heartworms. Because of this diversity, there is no one drug that will cure them all. If these worms are allowed to remain in the dog's system, they will eventually rob the dog of his stamina and produce a general deterioration, loss of weight, diarrhea, dulling of the coat, and vomiting. Due to this weakened condition, the dog also becomes susceptible to other diseases. Two of the most recognizable symptoms are a ravenous appetite without weight gain and a bloating of the stomach.

Roundworms. Roundworms commonly infect puppies, in whom they can cause lung and intestinal damage. The roundworm larvae enter the bloodstream by penetrating the intestinal lining and they are then carried to the lungs. Roundworms can commonly be seen in the feces. Their white cylindrical bodies are pointed at both ends. While they are generally small, they can be thread-like and up to three inches in length. Once roundworms reach the lungs, the dog will have a cough and may be threatened with pneumonia. Roundworms are excreted in the stool and transmitted when a dog comes in contact with contaminated soil. This is why strict sanitation is important so that the cycle of reinfection is broken after treatment for roundworms.

Tapeworms. Fleas, as intermediate hosts, are the most common source of tapeworms in dogs. By eliminating these external parasites, the incidence of tapeworm infestation will be greatly limited. The tapeworm is introduced into the dog's system when the dog bites at and swallows an infected flea or louse. The adult tapeworm attaches itself to the dog's intestinal wall and absorbs nutrients from his system, leaving him very hungry and in a weakened physical condition. Tapeworms may be difficult to eradicate, especially if the head of these segmented parasites remains embedded in the intestinal lining where it can regenerate. Several worming treatments, in this case, may need to be administered by the veterinarian in order to rid your dog of these pests. Over-the-counter tapeworm medications often produce unpleasant side effects, such as vomiting and diarrhea, so be sure to consult your veterinarian for the proper medicine.

Hookworms. If present in large quantities, hookworms can be deadly, as they attach themselves to the wall of the small intestine and, by sucking, remove blood from the dog. If they are left untreated, these bloodsuckers can cause circulatory collapse. Signs of hookworm infestation are diarrhea, anemia, weakness, and weight loss. Hookworms are very small, generally less than one-half inch in length, so detection without laboratory testing is rare. Hookworm larvae generally enter the dog's body by means of his ingesting larval worms off the ground; so, as always, good sanitation will help prevent further infection once treatment has been secured from your veterinarian. This includes properly disposing of all canine fecal matter in which the hookworm eggs have been deposited. Additionally, runs, kennels, and bedding should be disinfected regularly.

Whipworms. Like hookworms, whipworm larvae reach the dog's system through ingestion of larval worms from contaminated soil. In extreme cases symptoms are vomiting, diarrhea, and anemia, but in most cases whipworm infestation is mild and hard to detect. Routine examination for the presence of worms by your veterinarian will help prevent whipworms from going undetected.

Heartworms. The incidence of heartworm infestation in dogs, in the United States especially, has markedly increased in recent years. In its advanced stages, heartworm infestation can be life-threatening, as worms from six to twelve inches in length invade the heart in great numbers. An afflicted dog will have difficulty breathing, cough, tire easily, and lose weight despite a hearty appetite. In advanced cases the heart becomes so clogged with worms that it cannot pump enough blood to the various body organs.

The heartworm parasite is transmitted by mosquitoes who have previously fed off an infected dog. While it was once believed that heartworm infection occurred only in the southern areas of the United States, it has now been proven to occur wherever several species of mosquitoes live—this entails most of the North American continent.

While there is no preventive vaccine for heartworms, they can be avoided by administering daily doses of medication, particularly during the spring, summer, and fall months. If caught in the early stages, heartworm disease can be cured; but it is a slow, uncertain process and prevention by daily pill or liquid medication is strongly advised. The presence of heartworms can be confirmed by a blood test, so a yearly test (in late winter or early spring, before mosquito season) should be given. The preventive medicine, incidentally, will only be prescribed only if the dog proves to be worm-free. If your dog spends much time outdoors during warmer months when mosquitoes abound, it is especially important that you closely monitor him for the onset of heartworms. Early detection is vital.

EXTERNAL PARASITES

External parasites (fleas, ticks, lice, and mites) live on the dog's skin and feed on his blood, tissue fluid, and the skin itself. These parasites may cause irritations to the skin that progress into various infections and disorders. Besides causing problems themselves, some external parasites serve as carriers of disease or hosts for various internal parasites. Fleas, as previously mentioned, often carry tapeworms.

To avoid ectoparasitic infestations on your dog, you must routinely inspect his skin. Should he become infested, your veterinarian will be able to recommend a medicated shampoo or an appropriate treatment to help eliminate the parasites. The dog's bedding and environment must be cleaned regularly to prevent any embedded eggs from hatching and, thus, reinfecting the dog.

Mange. Parasites are responsible for two types of skin mange: sarcoptic and follicular. Sarcoptic mange is the most common form of this disorder, and it results in an intense skin irritation that causes the dog to scratch violently, often to the point of bloodying the skin. Upon investigation of the irritated skin, the veterinarian will find small red areas that have become engorged with pus. While sarcoptic mange can be controlled and eliminated with medicine provided by your veterinarian, this is a highly contagious condition and the afflicted dog should be kept isolated until he fully recovers.

Follicular mange, while much rarer than sarcoptic mange, is much more difficult to eliminate. The infection of the hair follicles leads to bare patches on the skin. These areas, rather than becoming tender and raw, often become thickened and leathery, which inhibits the hair from growing back in. Follicular mange is less contagious than its counterpart, but it is often a continual problem for an afflicted dog, as it is rarely eliminated in its entirety despite vigilant veterinary attention.

Ear Mites. These parasites live in the ear canal, feeding on skin debris. Signs of ear mites are large deposits of black or reddish brown ear wax, vigorous ear scratching, and head shaking.

155

Walnut Lanes Shao-Nu, owned by Ray Anderson **(top)**. Bedlam's Samantha, by Shir Du Sam Ku out of Bedlam's Stormy **(bottom)**. Ellen Weathers Debo, owner.

Veterinary inspection of the waxy discharge under a microscope will reveal the presence of ear mites. The first step in eliminating the problem is to thoroughly clean the wax from the ear canal. This must be done carefully and should be performed by a trained professional to avoid possible damage to the delicate tissues of the inner ear. If mites are discovered in the wax (wax is also a symptom of other ear disorders), your veterinarian will supply you with medicated ear drops. Through daily application of an ear mite medication, these pesky parasites will be eliminated in several weeks' time.

EMERGENCIES

Accidents, such as being hit by a car, are the most common emergency health situations experienced by dog owners. In an emergency, immediate action is called for to stabilize the injured dog until veterinary care is available. After being hit by a car, a dog should always be examined by a veterinarian for possible internal injuries—even if he appears unhurt.

Cuts, Wounds, and Fractures. In general, primary first aid for a dog is similar to that for a human. When ministering to a dog's wounds, one must be careful to avoid being bitten by the suffering animal. Even a normally docile dog, if painfully injured or badly frightened, is apt to bite anyone who comes near him. Before attempting to care for a severely injured dog in such a state, prepare a muzzle to secure his mouth. A man's necktie or a long strip of cloth will adequately serve this purpose. Begin by placing the midpoint of the cloth across the top of the dog's muzzle, crossing it under the lower jaw, bringing it up around the back of the neck, and tying it in a secure knot just behind and below the ears. This may be frightening to the dog, so talk to him soothingly throughout the procedure.

When dealing with a cut, begin by cleaning the area with a mild soap and hot water to reveal the site. If necessary, trim the hair around the cut so that you can get to the wound. If the wound is large enough to require bandaging, wrap some gauze around the area and get the dog to a veterinarian as soon as possible. Dogs are very adept at removing bandages, so let a professional prepare the dressing.

If the wound is in the head or neck area, you can keep the dog from scratching or licking it by applying an Elizabethan or cone collar. These lightweight collars can be easily constructed to temporarily inhibit the dog from getting to an injury. The collars can be made from cardboard and taped together or bound with thin cord.

Large wounds or ones in which the blood is continuously pouring forth will require pressure to halt the blood flow until veterinary care becomes available. Try to locate a pressure point near the injury to reduce the flow of blood to the area. Take a wad of cotton or a clean cloth and place it over the wound to serve as a pressure bandage. Tightly wrap some gauze over the cotton to hold it in place. In most cases, this should stop the flow of blood; if it doesn't, increase pressure by wrapping the gauze more tightly or by applying adhesive tape tightly over the gauze.

If the bleeding is very severe (perhaps an artery was cut), you will need to devise a tourniquet. Apply a tourniquet between the injury and the heart and twist the bandage until the blood flow is stopped. As with any major injury, time is really of the essence when a tourniquet is applied, as the flow of blood cannot be curtailed to an area for more than ten to fifteen minutes.

When dealing with a seriously injured dog, be sure to keep him as quiet as possible to avoid any further damage to internally injured organs. Talk soothingly and try to keep him as calm as possible. Do not move him unless he is still in danger or unless you need to transport him to a medical professional.

If you suspect that the dog has fractured some bones, restrain him from all movement. If there is a severe or compound fracture (the bone protruding from the wound), you may need to splint the break. In making such a splint, the main point to remember is that you want to keep the area steady, as any movement could cause possible nerve damage or an interruption to the blood supply. Transport the dog to the veterinarian as quickly as possible for immediate treatment.

Poisoning. If you suspect that your dog has swallowed a poisonous substance, first try to locate the source of the poison. If you find the container, read the label for instructions on how to deal with an accidental poisoning. The procedures can vary. To

158

These adorable puppies are three-week-old "miniature" Shar-peis **(top)**, and it is clear that they are free of eye entropion. A six-week-old youngster out of Bedlam's Mortisha **(bottom)**. Bred by the author.

induce vomiting may be the proper treatment in some cases of poisonings, but vomiting may be very damaging in other instances where the proper procedure may be to feed the dog milk or some other substance to help neutralize the poison's effects.

If your dog has been poisoned, you must act quickly. Notify your veterinarian of the problem by phone immediately, giving him as many details as possible so that he can prepare an antidote while you are rushing the dog to his office. He may offer some advice on how to care for the dog during the trip or ask you to administer a temporary treatment.

Worming medicines are major causes of poisoning in dogs. Well-meaning owners sometimes medicate their dogs with these preparations as a routine measure. When no worms are expelled, some people figure the dosage was not strong enough so they administer a second, stronger dose. Worming should be undertaken only when an infestation has been confirmed by your veterinarian and only under his guidance.

Other sources of poisonings in dogs are similar to those children often get into: carelessly placed cleaning agents, household products, and plants. Insecticides should be locked away securely. Car antifreeze that has dripped onto the street is surprisingly attractive to dogs, as it gives off a sweet fragrance. Be sure to monitor your dog when walking him to be sure he does not attempt to ingest such a material, as two tablespoons of antifreeze can cause severe kidney damage or death.

Burns. Allowing your dog free run of your house exposes him to many sources of burns: electric shock from biting cords, heat burns from too close contact with a fireplace or heater, or topical burns from overturned pots of hot water or oil in the kitchen.

With heat, or thermal burns, the immediate treatment is to apply cold water or ice compresses to the affected area. Clean the burn site with soap and cool water to remove any contaminants such as hair, dirt, or grass. Then rinse the area well, again with cool water. Avoid exposing the burned skin to the air by covering the area with cotton gauze or a loose bandage. If the burn is very severe, the dog may quickly lapse into shock. Keep him wrapped in a blanket and try to soothe him and keep him still while you get veterinary assistance.

160

Electric shock burns can be confined strictly to the mouth or they may affect the entire system. Only a veterinarian can properly handle such a situation, so contact him immediately and take the dog to him as quickly as possible. Even if the shock seems minor, there may be some damage to the mouth region that will require medication.

Insect Bites or Stings. While most insect bites are inconsequential and unknown to the dog owner, occasionally your dog may have an allergic reaction to a sting. This will generally be manifest in an outbreak of hives or other bumps on the skin. In minor cases such as this, examine the site of the sting and remove the stinger if you can find it.

In many rare cases your dog may have a severe reaction to the toxin from the sting. Danger signals are extreme swelling of the affected area and difficulty in breathing. Such a reaction is life-threatening and a veterinarian should be immediately contacted, as corticosteroids or other anti-inflammation drugs may need to be administered to halt the progression of the allergic reaction. Reactions such as this often follow a sting that occurred from the dog's snapping at and catching a bee or wasp in his mouth. Be alert to the possibility of such a dangerous sting if your dog is prone to this kind of behavior and correct him whenever you see him trying to catch insects. Keep in mind though that this natural instinct is hard to break.

Heatstroke. Heatstroke occurs most often in dogs that have been confined to a car or other small enclosure without proper ventilation on a warm day. It does not have to be 90°F outside for heatstroke to occur. A parked, poorly ventilated car can reach 100°F in a short amount of time on a relatively mild 75°F day. If you must leave your dog in the car for any reason, be sure to lower several windows at least three inches, leave a supply of water, and *make the confinement short*. If the dog is going to have to remain confined for any length of time, do everyone a favor and leave him home or take him along with you when you leave the car.

A change of climate can also induce heatstroke. Bringing a dog from a mild weather area to a hot climate without giving him time to adjust can put the dog into extreme physical stress. Very young or old dogs, as well as overweight dogs, are susceptible to heat stroke if they are allowed to exert themselves on hot days.

Down-Homes Un Long **(top)**. Down-Homes Clown Nosed Buddha, three times Best of Breed and Group I under Mr. Isidore Schoenberg, C. L. Savage, and Mrs. John B. Patterson (all United States judges); and Down-Homes Harmony, Best of Breed and Group II under Vincent Perry of the United States **(bottom)**. All dogs were bred by Matgo Law of Hong Kong.

162

Panting is the most obvious sign of heat stress. If this is coupled with an increased heart rate, agitation, and/or vomiting, contact your veterinarian immediately. He will probably advise you to take the dog's temperature rectally. If it is substantially elevated, he may have to be immersed in cool water immediately to break the upward progression of his temperature. If left unchecked, the dog can go into circulatory collapse and die. Treatment by your veterinarian will be required in all heat stress cases, as there are often secondary reactions that follow the initial temperature elevation.

Heatstroke can almost always be avoided by following some common sense rules. Always have a plentiful supply of water on hand, especially when travelling or on very hot days. Encourage your dog to take frequent small drinks. If you must place your dog in a carrier or confined area, supply him with some wet towels to help cool the area by evaporation. Never allow the dog to over-tax his system on a hot day, and take special care of overweight, old, or very young dogs. These dogs should be kept inside, out of the sun, if at all possible.

Snakebite. If your dog should tangle with a snake, first try to determine whether the snake was poisonous. Two fang marks usually indicate a poisonous bite, while a U-shaped row of teeth marks usually indicates a nonpoisonous bite. Should your dog be bitten by a poisonous snake, immediate action must be taken or paralysis and death can quickly follow. The first step is to calm and immobilize the dog, as exertion will further spread the venom in the dog's system. Such bites are very painful, so before you attempt to medicate your dog, muzzle him to prevent being bitten.

If the snakebite is on a leg, apply a tourniquet between the wound and the heart. It is not necessary to completely shut down the flow of blood, as with a severely bleeding wound, but to slow it dramatically. If possible, try to keep the bitten limb on a level that is horizontal with the heart to slow the movement of the venom through the bloodstream. If a veterinarian can reach the dog within ten minutes of the bite, this tourniquet generally will be enough to sustain him until the doctor can treat the wound and administer an antitoxin.

If there is no immediate veterinary attention available, you will need to open up the bite wound and try to remove as much of the poison from the area as possible. Use a sterilized sharp instrument (a knife or razor blade) and make two linear incisions above and below the wound to start the blood flowing. Apply suction (preferably not by mouth but with a suction cup) and get the dog to a veterinarian immediately. The dog will need immediate antitoxin, antibiotics, and pain killers.

Fire. Fire and smoke are life-threatening conditions for man and dog alike, and immediate evacuation from the burning area is the solution. However, many fires can occur when the owner is not at home and the dog is confined to the house or in a crate. Firemen will be unaware of the dog's presence unless they are alerted to it. Conscientious owners should post a decal in a prominent window that specifies the number of pets on the premises and the approximate area in which they can be found.

HEALTH DISORDERS

Dogs, like man, are susceptible to various disorders that can affect their quality of life. Advances in medicine and health care in recent years have gone far in increasing the knowledge of trained professionals in how to prevent, treat, and cure many of the most prevalent conditions.

Respiratory Infections. While viruses and bacteria are the true causes of such complaints as colds, bronchitis, and pneumonia, exposure to a draft after a bath, allowing a dog to sleep in the path of an air conditioner's current or near a radiator, and subjecting the dog to frequent temperature changes are man-made conditions that can affect the dog's overall health.

Sneezing, fever, water or pussy eyes, and a lack of appetite are common symptoms of respiratory infections. Mild cases involving a moderate amount of sneezing and a little eye discharge can generally be treated by keeping the dog warm, well-fed and watered, and inactive. If the discharges become pus-like and there are accompanying signs of dehydration, lack of appetite, and a persistent fever, veterinary care is in order. Antibiotics will generally be prescribed to counter the effect of the invading germs.

Constipation. While mild, temporary constipation can occur naturally in the dog due to changes in diet or as a reaction to cold, rainy weather (when the dog's thoughts are not on elimination out-of-doors but on getting back into the warmth of the house),

164

severe straining or a continued lack of bowel movements can indicate serious health problems, such as a tumor or an obstruction in the intestines.

If the condition seems mild, try increasing the amount of roughage in the dog's diet or add a small amount of mineral oil to his food once a day. The mineral oil supplements should not, however, be continued for more than three days, as the oil may interfere with the body's natural absorption of vitamins and minerals.

In more severe cases, consult your veterinarian. He may suggest such remedies as administering a mild dose of milk of magnesia as a laxative, or he may prescribe glycerine suppositories or an enema of warm water and mild soap.

Urine retention can also become a life-threatening condition if toxic substances are allowed to build up in the bladder and kidneys. If this condition continues for more than twenty-four hours, consult your veterinarian.

Hip Dysplasia. While this disorder is most common in the larger dog breeds, it can be found to affect all breeds. Hip dysplasia (HD) is a misalignment of the bones of the hip: the femur and the acetabulum. Generally, one of these bones is malformed and the surrounding tissues and ligaments cannot hold the bones in place. Either the acetabulum (socket) is too shallow and therefore cannot retain the head of the femur, causing slippage; or the head of the femur is flattened, which causes it to slip from the socket. The end result of this misfit is a stiffness in the rear legs and pain in movement.

Hip dysplasia exists in varying degrees of severity and is generally believed to be hereditary. While the condition is as yet incurable and uncorrectable by surgery, there is considerable study underway on how to eliminate this crippling disease. Medicines to alleviate the pain and reduce some of the inflammation and thereby allow the dog to move more naturally are available through veterinarians.

HD usually begins to noticeably affect a dog by two to six months of age. A dog displaying symptoms of HD should be X-rayed to determine the extent to which he is afflicted. Any dog that is diagnosed as having HD should never be used as breeding stock, as he can pass the disease along to his progeny. To avoid a

165

deterioration of the hip joint, it is also advised that the dog be restricted from climbing stairs and partaking in vigorous exercise, especially while growing, as this may increase the degeneration of the hip joints.

Eczema. Unlike other skin ailments, eczema is generally caused by improper nutrition rather than by a parasite. Eczema causes skin irritation and lesions to appear primarily along the back, especially in the tail region. It occurs mostly in the summer during hot, humid weather when the growth of bacteria is encouraged. A dog in a weakened condition is very susceptible to the invasion of this bacteria. The condition manifests itself in a small lesion, which the dog proceeds to spread by incessant scratching. Eczema is so irritating to the dog that he may scratch at himself until the lesion becomes bloody and raw. An antibiotic ointment will be needed to kill the bacteria and to relieve the itching. It is also advised to keep the dog free of fleas so that he won't scratch himself and in so doing spread the disease. A mild tranquilizer may have to be administered to control the frantic scratching.

A variant form of eczema called "hot spots" or "weeping mange" produces a moist infection and spreads very rapidly. It is not confined to the back and may infect many parts of the body. Along with the general symptoms of intense itching and bacterial infection may come vomiting, engorgement of the lymph nodes, and fever. An emollient to relieve itching and prevent further damage to the skin by scratching must be applied to the affected area after it has been thoroughly cleaned and clipped bare of fur. Your veterinarian will also prescribe an antibiotic and possibly an anti-inflammatory drug if the moist eczema has become severe.

Diabetes. As with humans, diabetes is a condition where there is an imbalance between the amount of sugar in the bloodstream and the amount of insulin that is produced to regulate the sugar usage. Because of the dog's inability to produce a sufficient amount of insulin, an excess amount of sugar remains in the blood. Symptoms are excessive thirst, weight loss, and frequent urination.

If left unchecked, diabetes can be fatal; however, great advances in curing this disease have taken place in recent years. Until a cure is perfected, there are very effective ways of controlling the disease. In severe cases insulin injections are prescribed, but in many instances close regulation of the diet can keep the diabetes under control.

166

TOOTH CARE

If tartar, or plaque, is allowed to build up at the gum line of your dog's teeth, this scaly deposit will eventually erode the tooth enamel, push the gums away from the teeth, and cause the teeth to loosen and fall out. To avoid such disastrous problems, periodically check the dog's teeth for signs of tartar. If you should notice a mild build-up of this material, brush his teeth once a week with a paste made from bicarbonate of soda and a little hydrogen peroxide. Apply the paste with a child's toothbrush or a gauze pad.

If the dog is prone to heavy tartar build-up, scraping the teeth will be necessary. This is best handled by your veterinarian, who may instruct you on how to carry this out at home if he feels this is a continuous problem.

If your dog develops offensive breath, this may be a sign of dirty or decaying teeth or diseased tonsils. If this condition persists for more than a few days, consult your veterinarian. A dental checkup is also in order if your dog shows a disinterest in eating for more than two days or if there are signs of redness, swelling, or sensitivity on the gums or in and around the mouth.

As with humans, a dog needs his teeth throughout his life. Take special care not to let them deteriorate unnecessarily or let them be injured through roughhousing. An easy way to wear off the points of your dog's teeth is to throw stones or other solid materials for your dog to retrieve. Specially designed toys and balls for dogs are the only items you should use for this type of game.

ALL DOGS NEED TO CHEW

Puppies and young dogs need something with resistance to chew on while their teeth and jaws are developing—for cutting the puppy teeth, to induce growth of the permanent teeth under the puppy teeth, to assist in getting rid of the puppy teeth at the proper time, to help the permanent teeth through the gums, to assure normal jaw development and to settle the permanent teeth solidly in the jaws.

The adult dog's desire to chew stems from the instinct for tooth cleaning, gum massage and jaw exercise—plus the need for an outlet for periodic doggie tensions.

This is why dogs, especially puppies and young dogs, will often destroy property worth hundreds of dollars when their chewing instinct is not diverted from their owner's possessions, particularly during the widely varying critical period for young dogs.

Saving your possessions from destruction, assuring proper development of teeth and jaws, providing for 'interim' tooth cleaning and gum massage, and channeling doggie tensions into a non-destructive outlet are, therefore, all dependent upon the dog having something suitable for chewing readily available when his instinct tells him to chew. If your purposes, and those of your dog, are to be accomplished, what you provide for chewing must be desirable from the doggie viewpoint, have the necessary functional qualities, and, above all, be safe for your dog.

It is very important that dogs not be permitted to chew on anything they can break or indigestible things from which they can bite sizeable chunks. Sharp pieces, such as from a bone which can be broken by a dog, may pierce the intestine wall and kill. Indigestible things which can be bitten off in chunks, such as toys made of rubber compound or cheap plastic, may cause an intestinal stoppage; if not regurgitated, they may bring painful death unless surgery is promptly performed.

Strong natural bones, such as 4 to 8 inch lengths of round shin bone from mature beef—either the kind you can get from your butcher or one of the variety available commercially in pet stores—may serve your dog's teething needs, if his mouth is large enough to handle them effectively.

You may be tempted to give your puppy a smaller bone and he may not be able to break it when you do—but puppies grow rapidly and the power of their jaws constantly increases until maturity. This means that a growing dog may break one of the smaller bones at any time, swallow the pieces and die painfully before you realize what is wrong.

Many people make the mistake of thinking of their dog's teeth in terms of the teeth of the wild carnivores or those of the dog in antiquity. The teeth of the wild carnivorous animals, and the teeth found in the fossils of the dog-like creatures of antiquity, have far thicker and stronger enamel than those of our contemporary dogs.

All hard natural bones are highly abrasive. If your dog is an avid chewer, natural bones may wear away his teeth prematurely; hence, they then should be taken away from your dog when the teething purposes have been served. The badly worn, and usually

168

Love those wrinkles on Oriental Treasure's Honey, a four-month-old owned and bred by Maryann Smithers of Boonton, New Jersey **(top).** Maryann also owns one-year-old Ch. Fingertail's Sterlings Ah Chu **(bottom),** bred by Jo Ann Webster, Fingertail Kennel, Raritan, New Jersey.

painful, teeth of many mature dogs can be traced to excessive chewing on natural bones.

Contrary to popular belief, knuckle bones which can be chewed up and swallowed by the dog provide little, if any, useable calcium or other nutriment. They do, however, disturb the digestion of most dogs and cause them to vomit the nourishing food they need.

Dried rawhide products of various types, shapes, sizes and prices are available on the market and have become quite popular. However, they don't serve the primary chewing functions very well; they are a bit messy when wet from mouthing, and most dogs chew them up rather rapidly—but they have been considered safe for dogs until recently. Now, more and more incidents of death, and near death, by strangulation have been reported to be the result of partially swallowed chunks of rawhide swelling in the throat. More recently, some veterinarians have been attributing cases of acute constipation to large pieces of incompletely digested rawhide in the intestine.

The nylon bones, especially those with natural meat and bone fractions added, are probably the most complete, safe and economical answer to the chewing need. Dogs cannot break them or bite off sizeable chunks; hence, they are completely safe—and being longer lasting than other things offered for the purpose, they are economical.

Hard chewing raises little bristle-like projections on the surface of the nylon bones—to provide effective interim tooth cleaning and vigorous gum massage, much in the same way your tooth brush does it for you. The little projections are raked off and swallowed in the form of thin shavings—but the chemistry of the nylon is such that they break down in the stomach fluids and pass through without effect.

The toughness of the nylon provides the strong chewing resistance needed for important jaw exercise and effective help for the teething functions—but there is no tooth wear because nylon is so non-abrasive. Being inert, nylon does not support the growth of microorganisms—and it can be washed in soap and water, or it can be sterilized by boiling or in an autoclave.

Nylabone® is highly recommended by veterinarians as a safe, healthy nylon bone that can't splinter or chip. Instead, Nylabone is frizzled by the dog's chewing action, creating a toothbrush-like

170

Tai Seng's Fingertail Fudge, a chocolate and producer of chocolate puppies. He is owned by Jo Ann Webster of Fingtertail Kennel, Raritan, New Jersey.

surface that cleanses the teeth and massages the gums. Nylabone® and Nylaball®, the only chew products made of flavor-impregnated solid nylon, are available in your local pet shop.

Nothing, however, substitutes for periodic professional attention to your dog's teeth and gums, not any more than your toothbrush can do that for you. Have your dog's teeth cleaned by your veterinarian at least once a year, twice a year is better—and he will be healthier, happier and far more pleasant to live with.

Bedlam's White Magic, a three-week-old who will need corrective surgery on his left eye. Anyone thinking about breeding Shar-peis should be aware of eye entropion (inrolling of the eyelids), which is an ocular defect often seen in this breed.

172

Chapter 8

Breeding

Each year millions of unwanted dogs are destroyed. While the majority of these dogs are mongrels—products of unplanned matings—there have been a great many purebred dogs whose outcome has been similar, largely because of their owners' ignorance and carelessness. As the owner of a purebred dog, or of *any* dog for that matter, you must decide carefully whether there is a need and a place for the puppies that your dog's breeding may bring forth. In other words, if you plan to breed your dog, you must ensure (preferably beforehand) that homes will be found for each puppy. Breeding purebred dogs should never be thought of as a "get-rich-quick" scheme; on the contrary, properly raising and caring for a litter of pups requires a significant investment of time and money. It is hard work, yet it can be fun and satisfying.

SHOULD I SPAY MY DOG?
The decision to spay or neuter your dog usually is made while the dog is still a puppy and generally applies only to the female, or bitch. Male dogs are almost never neutered, unless they are overly aggressive or exhibit excessive sexual tendencies. Females, however, experience regular heat cycles approximately every six months, during which time they are able (and generally eager) to conceive. As the owner of a female, you must decide whether you want to raise a litter of puppies, and, if not, whether you want to

173

deal with preventing an unwanted mating each time the dog comes into heat. If breeding is not in your plans, spaying is a permanent solution. Performed by a veterinarian, it is a relatively riskless operation that will not affect the dog's personality or physical condition throughout her life. If, however, you intend to show your dog in competition, spaying cannot be performed since by some regulating organizations it is viewed as a disqualification.

Spaying is generally performed after the dog has had her first heat cycle but before her first birthday. At this age she has attained her female characteristics and is in excellent condition. Spaying involves the removal of both ovaries, thus it is impossible for the dog to have puppies or come into season (heat).

SHOULD I BREED MY DOG?

While almost any two healthy dogs can mate and produce puppies, the decision to breed a dog should be well thought out in advance. Bringing forth puppies of good quality—ones that enhance rather than detract from the overall quality of the breed— should be the goal of each and every mating. Haphazard matings of easily available dogs generally produce offspring of similar or inferior quality than the parents. While such matings undoubtedly can result in lovable puppies, this is not the way to breed better dogs. As there is already a plethora of puppies, breedings should be planned on the basis of a dog's ancestry and on established scientific principles.

The main rule followed by knowledgeable breeders is to breed only the best specimen to the best partner. A thorough, accurate knowledge of the breed standard imparts an image of what the perfect specimen of the breed should look like. Of course few, if any, perfect specimens of a breed exist, but knowing what to look for in your dog and its prospective mate is a *must* in determining whether or not to breed your dog. If you are ever in doubt about the quality of your potential brood bitch or stud dog, ask an experienced breeder for his or her evaluation and advice.

PEDIGREES

A dog's pedigree can be an effective tool in aiding a breeder to produce better dogs—if enough is known about the dog's ancestors to supply information on their genetic makeup, that is. This is one reason why it is strongly suggested that if you are interested in breeding you purchase the best quality specimen possible from an established kennel. Because established breeders tend to keep exacting records of their matings and puppies, you should be able to find information about the strengths and weaknesses of your dog's descendants—if you are willing and interested enough to search and ask questions.

When you purchased your puppy, you may have been given a copy of your dog's pedigree. If not, most breeders would be happy to supply you with one if it is requested. Most pedigrees go back three generations; but one with five generations is valuable as it contains information on sixty dogs. This listing of your dog's close relatives can tell you more than just the names of his ancestors. It can also indicate the breeding strategies (linebreeding, inbreeding, outcrossing, outbreeding) followed by the breeder.

When investigating your dog's pedigree, bear in mind that while the names of champions may appear throughout your dog's ancestry, this is no guarantee that the offspring will be of superior quality. Show-quality dogs often produce pet-quality progeny. The traits transmitted to a puppy depend on the genetic structure that he inherits from his parents and their parents before him. To understand the factor of probability involved in breeding dogs, it is strongly suggested that a prospective breeder have a working knowledge of genetic principles and how they relate to dog breeding.

THE MECHANICS OF GENETICS

The passage of traits or characteristics from parent to offspring does not occur in a haphazard manner. It is a matter of genetic inheritance. The science of genetics traces back to the work of an Austrian monk named Gregor Mendel who discovered that there is a reliable method of inheritance that can be predicted. Mendel found that small units, called *genes*, are present in the cells of all individuals. These genes control the development of the organism's characteristics. They are present in pairs, with one half of each pair being inherited from each parent. When each half of the partner genes was found to affect the organism in an identical manner, the pair was called *homozygous*. When each half of the pair was found to affect the organism in a contrasting manner, the pair was called *heterozygous*.

Mendel discovered that in heterozygous gene pairs containing contrasting characteristics, one half of the pair suppresses the characteristics contained in the other half of the pair. He termed the characteristic that expresses itself *dominant,* and the one that remained hidden he termed *recessive.* There are instances, however, when neither gene is completely dominant over the other. This is known as *incomplete or partial dominance* and the result is a blending of the characteristics from the pair. A few examples of traits that are genetically dominant and recessive in dogs are as follows:

Dominant	Recessive
Dark eyes	Light eyes
Brown eyes	Blue eyes
Short coat	Long coat
Wire coat	Smooth coat
Curly coat	Straight coat
Large ears	Small ears
Long ears	Short ears
Low set ears	High set ears
Erect ears	Dropped ears
High set tail	Low set tail
Black nose	Dudley nose
Short foreface	Long foreface
Long head	Short head

To put these principles to work in breeding better dogs, breeders must understand that what a dog looks like physically, or on the outside, does not directly reflect what he looks like genetically, on the inside. His outward appearance is his *phenotype,* and all the traits he has inherited from his ancestors that he can pass on to his offspring form his *genotype.* Phenotype is not a guarantee of genotype. In other words, what a dog looks and acts like is no guarantee that he can pass these traits on to his offspring. This is even further complicated by the fact that some traits (phenotypes) are the result of several genes and therefore difficult to predict.

176

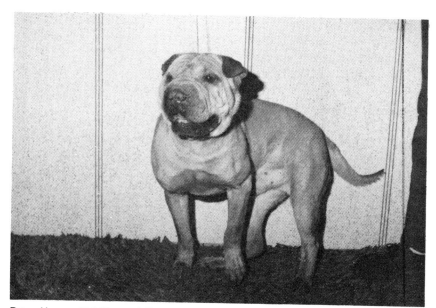

Down-Homes Hoi-Chee of Eshaf, sire of Quen Yen and Hoi-Ti and owned by the Fahses of Eshaf's Kennels, Cicero, Illinois **(top).** Bedlam Kennels' Down-Homes Oriental Pearl with her first litter of seven pups **(bottom).** Note the number of color varieties in one litter.

1. Two dominant genes: he is pure for that trait, having received a dominant gene from each parent. This is termed *dominant/homozygous*.
2. Two recessive genes: he is pure for that trait, having received a recessive gene from each parent. This is termed *recessive/homozygous*.
3. One dominant and one recessive gene: he is mixed for that trait, having received a dominant gene from one parent and a recessive gene from the other. This is termed *heterozygous*.

By applying these (simplified) principles, there is a ratio that can be applied to help predict the genotype of the offspring of a mating. If a parent is homozygous for a trait (1 and 2), he will pass on that trait regardless of which half of his gene pair he gives to the offspring. If a parent is heterozygous for a trait (3), he will pass on either a dominant or a recessive gene to his offspring—a 50/50 chance. These ratios apply for both parents, and whether or not an offspring exhibits a trait depends on the number of dominant and recessive genes he receives from each half of the inherited gene pairs. There are six ways that a pair of genes can unite, based on the possible combinations of dominance and recessiveness present in the genotype of the sire and dam.

The task facing a dedicated breeder is to determine what genes are present in his breeding stock and to plan matings that will bring forth offspring which exhibit and carry desirable genes. The goal is to eliminate unwanted traits not only from the phenotype but also from the genotype of future generations. In this way the overall quality of the breed should improve. The breeding out of undesirable characteristics can be successful if sires and dams are selected carefully, using various breeding strategies to find mates that complement each other. It is important to choose a mate who shows strengths where his partner shows weaknesses, an animal whose background is compatible with that of his partner's.

Linebreeding. This is the process whereby dogs of fairly close relationship are mated in order to eliminate faults and "fix" a uniform type in the offspring by increasing the homozygosity of the gene pairs. Linebreeding usually involves mating dogs that share a common ancestor but that are not closely related themselves. The potential sire and dam should both contain a common ancestor in

178

their second or third generation. This ancestor should be of superior quality, known to pass on his quality to his offspring. Through linebreeding correct type is set and maintained through several generations, and it is the system most recommended by experienced breeders.

Inbreeding. This is a strategy whereby closely related dogs are mated: dam to son, sire to daughter, brother to sister, or half-brother to half-sister. This system is generally used only by experienced breeders who have a good knowledge of the genotypes of the dogs being considered for a mating and know that certain genes are present that they want to concentrate in the offspring. It is also used to expose faults in the breeding line and thereby eliminate them (by eliminating the carriers) from further matings. Because this system concentrates and fixes type very quickly, inferior pups are often produced that must be culled. This system should not be employed very often; when it is, it should not be used by novices.

Outcrossing. Unlike linebreeding, which tries to increase the homozygosity of the gene pairs, outcrossing is a system by which new genes are introduced to increase the heterozygosity of the gene pool. To accomplish this, mates are selected that complement each other while not sharing any common ancestors within at least the last five generations. The breeder is deliberately attempting to add some new, desirable trait or traits to compensate for qualities that are lacking in his breeding stock. The sire or dam selected for the outcross should most likely be the product of linebreeding and thereby exhibit strong prepotency for the traits needed in the breeding program. Outcrossing should be attempted only sparingly, when a specific need is quoted in the breeding program. Once outcrossing is accomplished, breeders generally breed the offspring to a linebreeding plan.

Outbreeding. This is really the unsystematic approach to breeding, the pattern followed by most well-meaning novices who mate their purebred dogs to any available purebred that is easily accessible. Often the ancestry of the sire and dam are unknown and they most likely share no common relatives. There is a high level of heterozygosity and the offspring are generally genetically inferior specimens. Outbreeding should not be confused with

Ausables China Love, also known as "Pickles," toward the end of her pregnancy **(top)**. She is beginning to "blow her coat," and unfortunately she has had skin problems, as have many of the lighter-colored cream Shar-peis. Owner, Ellen Weathers Debo. Ch. Bedlam's Panda, C.D. **(bottom)** with her litter of nine puppies. Breeder/owner, Maryann Smithers of Oriental Treasure Kennel.

crossbreeding, which is the mating of distinct breeds—the products of which are mongrels. Outbreeding rarely produces show-quality animals and does little for the breed except bring forth puppies. As there is generally an overabundance of such puppies, outbreeding is the system knowledgeable breeders would most like eliminated.

BREEDING BETTER DOGS

As mentioned in the preceding genetics section, breeding better dogs is based on a number of factors: a good basic breeding stock, a working knowledge of genetics, patience, and a little luck. Whatever system of breeding is used, the point to remember is to breed only the best to the best—and then hope for the best! The concerted efforts of breeders who conduct their breeding programs with an eye for improving the breed and attaining the "perfect" specimen should be encouraged and praised, as in this lies the hope for the future. The haphazard, careless breedings of pet stock should be discouraged and prevented whenever possible, as the products of these matings seldom improve the overall quality of the breed.

THE REPRODUCTIVE CYCLE

The female dog, commonly referred to as the "bitch," usually reaches sexual maturity at nine months of age, although this can vary from as early as six months to as late as twelve. At this time she begins her heat cycle (also referred to as her "season" or the estrus period) which lasts approximately twenty-one days.

There are various stages in the heat cycle. Prior to its onset, the female is restless and exhibits an increased appetite. This preheat period generally lasts about five days, during which time the vulva begins to swell, often to several times its normal size. This period is followed by the onset of heat, which is characterized by a bloody discharge that lasts for several days and then begins to diminish. Approximately nine days after the first signs of discharge, the dog becomes playful with other dogs. However, she will not accept a male for mating until a few days later, around days eleven through eighteen of the heat cycle. At this time she will become quite aggressive and seek out a male for mating. As the cycle proceeds (days nineteen through twenty-one) she will still be attractive to males but will no longer permit a mating. This mating cycle can vary quite markedly from dog to dog and breed to breed;

but it is still characterized by the various phases. The heat cycle occurs approximately every six months, although this can vary among bitches.

The male dog, commonly called the "stud," usually reaches sexual maturity at six to eight months of age. Unlike the female, the male dog is able to breed at any time of the year. He does not experience the so-called heat cycles.

CARING FOR THE BITCH IN SEASON

Should you decide to breed your female, you should not attempt this until at least her second or third heat. The bitch is still growing at the time of the first heat, and she is not physically prepared for the rigors of raising a litter. To prevent an unspayed female from mating during her heat period, you will need to take some precautions.

Never leave her unattended outside, even if tied, as males will go to great lengths to get to her. This is especially important in the middle of her cycle when she will accept and encourage a mating. To prevent the local males from discovering that she is in heat, you should take her away from her immediate surroundings to relieve herself, as the urine of a bitch in heat gives off a scent that is particularly attractive to male dogs. It is best to take her out in the car to a park or public spot, being very careful, always, to contain her on a leash and clean up all solid wastes. This may sound like a lot of trouble, but it may keep the male dogs from congregating around your house in the hopes of getting to your bitch.

Many people feel it is easier to board the female in heat at a local kennel until the season is over, but this is by far the most expensive alternative. If you should choose such an option, be sure to make it clear that the female is in heat and must be kept separated from all males.

Your veterinarian can supply you with pills that will reduce the odor of the urine during the heat period. There are also other items on the market to prevent the bloody discharge from staining household items or clothes, although most females in heat are very meticulous and tend to keep their genitals very clean.

Spaying is the permanent alternative for preventing a mating and should be considered if other preventive methods seem troublesome.

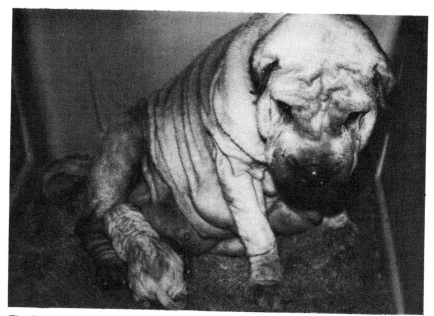

The first born in this litter has already started to nurse **(top).** If the litter is a large one and there aren't enough nipples to go around, or if the bitch has trouble producing milk, you may have to supplement her supply by hand feeding with a bottle or by tube feeding. As the bitch contracts, another littermate **(bottom)** emerges in its fluid-filled amniotic sac.

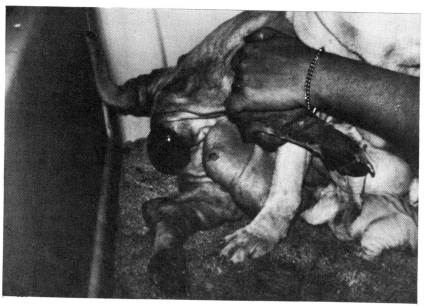

183

THE MATING

Once you have decided that you want to raise a litter of puppies and have selected suitable mates, you should prepare the dogs for the mating. First and foremost, both dogs—but especially the bitch—must be in very good physical condition. They should be checked for worms and other diseases before the breeding, as these can be passed on to the puppies by the bitch. The animal must be free of disease before she is allowed to beget a litter of pups.

Even though the two dogs will know instinctively how to mate, the breeder should still be present to monitor the proceedings. Once the male has penetrated the female, pressure on the penis causes a reflex action that fills a bulbous enlargement at the base of the penis. This bulb swells to five times its normal size within the female, locking the two animals together. This is called the "tie" and the animals usually remain tied together for fifteen to thirty minutes after the male ejaculates. The breeder must supervise to prevent a sudden attempt by either dog to pull away, as this could result in serious injury—both physical and emotional—to either the stud or bitch.

THE STUD FEE

Prior to the mating, settle *in writing* the terms of the stud service. The owner of the stud usually charges a fee, but he or she may instead prefer to take a puppy from the resultant litter. This may be the "pick of the litter" (first selection) or a second or third choice, which allows the owner of the bitch to make the first selection. While the payment of a stud fee does not in itself guarantee a litter, it does generally confer the right to breed the bitch and stud again at her next season in the event no puppies be born from the first mating.

The agreement should be precisely stated, including such details as at what age the selection of puppies should be made and what happens if only one puppy is produced from the mating.

PREGNANCY

The average gestation period for dogs is sixty-three days, although this may vary a week in either direction. Bitches expecting large litters often whelp a little early, while a small litter may go a few days overdue.

The first breeding can be traumatic and have a detrimental effect on a young stud dog if all should not go well, so it is important to reassure him and praise him constantly **(top).** The mating of dogs is not a sideshow or a spectator sport; only one or two persons should be present to lend a helping hand **(bottom).**

185

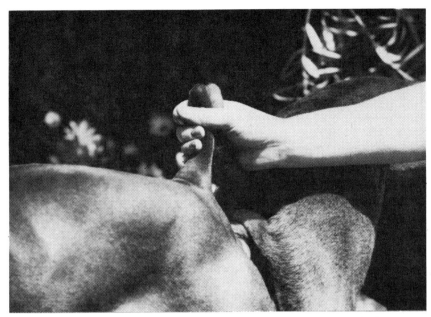

Never turn a stud dog and bitch loose during mating and let nature just take its course. At least one person should be present to hold the two dogs together until the "tie" is complete **(top).** Bedlam's Yo Ki Hi **(bottom)** nurses her litter. Make sure the bitch gets plenty of food and water after whelping—let her eat all she wants.

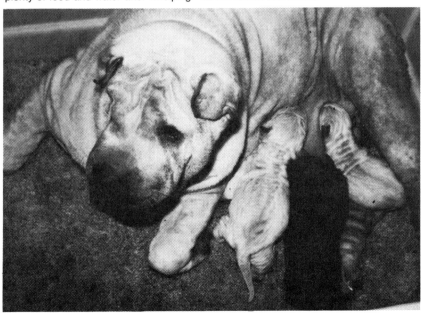

Signs of pregnancy are hard to detect, although many bitches tend to lose their appetite or vomit a week or so after the mating, indicating an upset stomach due to hormone change. Aside from this, there will be no real noticeable physical changes in the bitch until the fourth or fifth week. At this time the bitch will begin to show an expanding abdomen and enlarged nipples with a color change. A clear discharge will usually appear around the fifth week and continue through the birth of the puppies. This should be washed off, at least once a day, with a mild soap and warm water solution.

Throughout the pregnancy you should supplement the bitch's meals with vitamins and minerals to help her maintain her strength and to whelp more easily. Your veterinarian can prescribe the appropriate dosages.

The puppies grow considerably in the last three weeks before birth, so the mother must be made to eat a sufficient, well- balanced diet during this high-growth period. At this time she will have little spare room in the abdomen and may require smaller portions given at more frequent intervals. If she should refuse her food, tempt her with her favorite treats or with pieces of chicken or liver to stimulate the appetite.

While exercise is important throughout the pregnancy, strenuous exercise should be avoided as she nears the final weeks. Take her for leisurely walks at least twice a day to help her maintain muscle tone and to keep up her strength. Discourage her from doing any jumping or from climbing a lot of stairs, which could induce early labor.

PREPARING FOR THE PUPPIES

Approximately a week before the puppies are due, you should prepare a whelping box and the area to which the mother and pups will be confined. Choose a location that is warm, well lit, and fairly quiet. For ease and cleanliness, it is best if the area is close to a source of water. Allow the bitch to investigate and become accustomed to this birthing area and encourage her to sleep there prior to the actual birth.

A whelping box is needed for the birth of the litter and for the first few weeks of their life. Introduce the bitch to her box before the birth so that she will feel comfortable with it and will therefore use it (rather than making a nest in your bed or in some other inappropriate spot). Whether you purchase a whelping box or construct your own, keep in mind that it should not be too big. It should be large enough to allow the bitch to lay comfortably but not so large that she cannot reach the sides when stretching out. During labor most bitches like to push against the sides of the whelping box with their legs to aid in the delivery of the puppies. After the birth, a fairly snug box will aid in keeping the pups warm and near the dam, rather than letting them move away from the security of their mother.

The size of the box will depend on the size of the bitch. The sides should be at least high enough to keep the puppies inside, while at the same time low enough to allow the mother to get out after she has nursed her brood. The sides also prevents drafts from chilling the puppies. In cold weather, it is advisable to raise the box an inch or so off the floor to further protect against drafts.

Inside the box you should construct a guard rail two or three inches from the bottom to allow the puppies space to crawl. This will prevent the mother from rolling over on them and possibly smothering them accidentally. This rail should be made of wood and should extend out far enough so as to keep the bitch from pressing against the sides of the box.

The base of the whelping box should be covered with several layers of newspapers. These paper layers will absorb any fluids expelled during the whelping and they can be easily changed. Some breeders line the bottom of the box with carpeting to make it more comfortable and then place the newspapers on top. Once the puppies are a few days old, remove the newspapers and insert a soft towel or blanket instead. This new surface will offer the puppies more traction as they begin to climb around, and it will be more comfortable for all. The bedding should be removed daily and laundered. Be sure to secure any large piece of bedding to protect the puppies from getting tangled in it or from possibly suffocating in the loose material.

WHELPING SUPPLIES

Prior to the birth, set up a tray or table with all the supplies you will need during the whelping. You should have these items close at hand: a few small terry cloth towels or washcloths, soap,

188

iodine, a small pair of blunt-tipped scissors, alcohol (to keep the scissors sterile), a thermometer, sterile gauze pads, white thread, a waste container, a small box lined with towels for the puppies, and a heating pad or hot water bottle to keep the puppy box warm. A scale for weighing each puppy at birth is also recommended.

The small box for the puppies is used between births. Be sure that it is adequately lined with soft, absorbent material and that it is kept warm. When placing the puppies in the box, be sure they are dry. The puppies are temporarily removed from the whelping box because their dam may become preoccupied with the next birth and, therefore, may accidentally injure the newborns. The removal should be done carefully so as not to upset the dam, and the box containing the puppies should be kept within her sight.

If possible, raise the temperature in the whelping room to 80°F. Keep a room thermometer near the whelping box to monitor the temperature in the puppies' environment. It is recommended that the whelping box be maintained at 85°F for the first two weeks.

WHELPING

As the time for whelping nears, try to spend as much time as possible with the bitch to comfort her. She may exhibit some early signs that labor is imminent, such as digging, tearing newspaper, and generally acting restless. A drop in temperature to approximately 99°F is a true indication that whelping will begin in the next twelve to twenty-four hours. You should begin monitoring the bitch's temperament several days before she is due to be aware of any change in pattern. Should her temperature fall below 99°F and remain constant for more than twenty-four hours without any signs of labor, contact your veterinarian, as she may be in need of medical attention. Alternatively, should her temperature rise to more than 102°F, you should consult your veterinarian, as an infection may be present.

The birth process will take place in three stages: (1) the early labor and dilation of the uterine passages, (2) the contractions and eventual expulsion of the whelp, and (3) the expulsion of the afterbirth (one for each puppy).

Remain with the bitch throughout the birth, but interfere only when absolutely necessary. Should the bitch appear to be having severe contractions for more than an hour without producing a whelp, veterinary attention should be sought before the dog reaches the point of exhaustion, which endangers the lives of both the whelps and the bitch.

The whelp generally will be presented head first, but feet first presentation (breech birth) is also common. Once the whelp begins to emerge, it should take only a few more contractions and pushes from the dam to eject it. Let the dam do the work. If she seems to abandon the pup or fail to remove the membrane covering the puppy's head, you must then take over and tear it open. Once the puppy is delivered, the mother will lick her newborn to dry and stimulate it. Should she fail in this, place the whelp in a clean, rough towel. Rub the pup briskly, holding it with its head pointed downward to help drain any fluids that may be present in the lungs. Then gently clean out the pup's mouth with a gauze pad or cotton swab to remove all mucus.

The placenta (afterbirth) is usually expelled immediately after the whelp, but it may be retained for up to ten minutes. Make sure it is expelled, as a retained afterbirth can cause serious infection. Once the placenta has been passed, the mother will bite and sever the umbilical cord; she may then eat the afterbirth. The afterbirth, incidentally, contains a generous supply of vitamins and minerals, as well as a hormone that aids in uterine contraction and stimulates milk production. Allow the dam to eat one or two of these. Remove all others, however, as the afterbirth also contains a laxative that can be detrimental in large amounts.

If the umbilical cord is wrapped around the whelp's neck or if the dam fails to bite the cord, you must rectify these situations. If the latter occurs, hold the afterbirth above the whelp; allow any fluid in the umbilical cord to drain to the puppy, as it is rich in nutrients. Using a piece of cotton thread, tie a knot about one inch from the whelp's body. Use the blunt-tipped scissors and cut directly above the knot. Apply a few drops of iodine to the umbilical stub to help disinfect it, and then return the puppy to its mother.

The whelps should be encouraged to begin nursing immediately after birth. If they do not naturally find their way to a teat, place them there and stroke them to encourage their nursing instincts. The pups should be taken away only when the birth of another whelp is imminent, and they should be placed in the warm puppy

190

box until the birth is complete. The nursing of the pups will encourage the dam's milk production. Supplementation with puppy formula should not be attempted for at least several days, unless a problem arises with the dam's milk supply.

The birth of each whelp should occur at regular intervals, but the pattern will vary with each dam and each whelping—from five minutes to several hours apart. Once you believe all the pups have been whelped, have the dam examined by your veterinarian to make sure she is in good condition and that all pups and afterbirths have been expelled. The veterinarian will most likely give her an injection of calcium and vitamin D, which helps prevent eclampsia, and a dose of hormone to help clean out the uterus.

The veterinarian usually will give the puppies a quick examination for general condition. If all is in order, leave the dam and pups alone for several hours to rest and regain their strength. Return in several hours and encourage the dam to leave the whelping box to relieve herself. You should then clean up the box and attend to the dam, since she might need a quick wash. While she is out of her box, give her a drink of water and a small offering of food.

Try to establish a daily, and later a weekly, pattern of checking on the growth of the puppies. Weigh each one shortly after birth and then again two days later. There should be a slight weight increase. If no gain is seen in several days, consult your veterinarian. As each pup matures, observe its overall health and growth patterns (the bite, eyes, testicles, legs, etc.). Be sure to clip the puppies's nails as soon as they begin to grow; otherwise the pups may scratch and irritate their dam as they nurse.

CAESAREAN SECTION

Caesarean sections are usually resorted to after the dam has been in hard labor for several hours without producing a whelp. It is essential that dogs not be allowed to labor too long, until they reach a point of exhaustion, as this tremendously increases their chances of going into shock and not surviving the operation. The fruitless labor is often the result of a pelvis that is too shallow to allow passage of the whelp, an unusual presentation of the whelp, or a toxic or life-threatening condition for either the dam or her whelps.

A Caesarean section involves cutting through the walls of the dam's abdomen and uterus to remove the puppies. In recent years there have been great advances in the types of anesthetics used and the methods for administering them, making the risk to the dam minimal—provided she is not in an overly exhausted condition. During a Caesarean birth, the puppies are affected by the anesthetic given to the dam and they are often slow to begin breathing once removed from the womb. Should this occur, artificial respiration, as well as brisk rubbing, will induce breathing. It is imperative that the puppies be kept warm after birth, and it is advisable to place a heating pad set on low or a hot water bottle in the whelping box with the mother and whelps to provide a little extra warmth. The puppies should not, however, be allowed to return to the mother until she is alert and free of the effects of the anesthetic.

Despite a discomfort in the now-stitched abdominal region, the new mother will want her pups near her and nursing to begin. While the milk flow may be temporarily delayed after a Caesarean section, the suckling of the puppies will quickly stimulate milk production. The mother should be closely monitored for the next few days—her temperature taken twice daily—to make sure an infection does not occur. Should her temperature rise to over 102°F, a veterinarian should be consulted immediately. The stitches should be examined daily for signs of inflammation and she should be kept very clean during the healing process. The bedding should be removed and laundered daily.

POSTPARTUM CARE

The dam will insist on remaining close to her whelps for the first week, generally leaving only to relieve herself. As the pups grow in strength, she may leave for more extended periods. During this time she will not want interruptions from strangers, so try to keep her as isolated as possible.

Keep a fresh supply of water available at all times. She will want little of this in the first twenty-four hours, but broth is usually an enticement she won't refuse. Offer her milk several times a day, since she needs as much fluid intake as possible to help with her own milk supply. She can be given small portions of solid food after the first day, such as ground beef or chicken. She will

Puppies often snuggle up for security and to keep warm **(top).** These eight-week-old pups were bred by Maryann Smithers of Oriental Treasure Kennel, Boonton, New Jersey. Occasionally a puppy develops an umbilical hernia at birth **(bottom).** If this happens, the rupture may have to be closed surgically.

193

soon need little tempting to eat, as she will have a ravenous appetite to make up for the calories expended during nursing. She will need two large meals a day, and a supply of dry food should be made available to her at all times. Her diet should be high in protein and calcium.

ECLAMPSIA

Eclampsia, or "milk fever," is a convulsive condition that is caused by a low calcium content in the bitch's blood. It can occur in late pregnancy or during the nursing period, and it is a life-threatening condition.

Symptoms are nervousness, a stiffening of the legs, pale gums, and excessive panting. Onset of the disease is often not obvious. Upon noticing a temperature increase to 102°F, veterinary attention should be sought immediately. An onset of eclampsia will require an injection of calcium and vitamin D, which enables the body to utilize and absorb the calcium.

If eclampsia is suspected, the puppies must be removed from the dam to prevent a further loss of calcium due to nursing.

MASTITIS

This condition is an inflammation of the mammary glands, caused by an excess of milk. As milk accumulates, the gland becomes congested and painful for the dam. It occurs because the gland is not being thoroughly drained, often due to weak suckling or due to small litters that are unable to attend to all the tests equally.

If left uncorrected, mastitis can lead to a bacterial infection which requires antibiotics. Once the condition is indicated, treat the inflamed teat either by placing a pup on it to more fully empty it or by gently hand-expressing the milk. By careful rotation of the puppies, mastitis can be quickly cleared up.

RECORDKEEPING

During the birth process have a notebook handy to record important information regarding the whelping. Take care to monitor the vital signs of the bitch and make note of any unusual patterns or problems that may arise. This data may be helpful later on (for your veterinarian) should the bitch develop any complications.

194

Document the birth of each pup and the expulsion of its after-birth. Later, transfer your notes onto a separate card for each puppy and maintain a master register of all your information. This will prove valuable whenever you need to evaluate a particular litter or your overall breeding plan. You may also want to pass on all pertinent information to the new owners of the puppies that you sell.

The following details should be recorded for each litter:

- name of the dam and sire
- date of mating
- approximate due date
- actual whelping date
- length of whelping (for each puppy)
- problems of the dam in whelping
- number of puppies in litter
- sex ratio of puppies
- defects or deaths in the litter
- evaluation of the puppies (made at several weeks of age)

The following details should be recorded for each puppy:

- birth weight
- problems at birth
- date of birth
- litter registration number
- registration numbers of dam and sire
- identifying marks
- date sold
- price
- conditions of sale
- name, address, and telephone number of new owner
- name of dog (if given)

Six-week-old Loong Ch'ai Merlin, bred and owned by Betsy Davison of Sarasota, Florida. Remember that the Shar-pei is not the breed for everyone. It has inherited the Chow Chow's loyal disposition and can become very attached to one person in particular; so, before you fall in love with a cute wrinkly puppy, make certain that you can provide the secure and loving environment it needs.

Chapter 9

Puppy Care

Before your puppy is able to take his place in your home, he will have gone through many formative stages that help shape his later character traits and habits. The following transitional stages mark his early growth.

From birth to two weeks of age the puppy's needs are simple: warmth, food from his dam, and lots of sleep. The ears begin to function at around ten days and the eyes open at ten to fourteen days. During this stage people should talk softly and stroke the puppy but avoid trying to pick him up or separate him from his mother.

At three to four weeks of age the puppy takes his first steps and begins to interact with his littermates. He begins to vocalize and investigate his immediate surroundings. During this stage, the puppy can be held and exposed to the noises of the household. His first supplementary food can be introduced into the diet, thereby beginning the weaning process.

At five to seven weeks of age the puppy is getting his first lessons in self-control. Weaning continues and the mother begins teaching him discipline and manners. The puppy is starting to enjoy actively socializing with his littermates and with humans. This is a vital stage in the puppy's character development, as exposure to various people and situations prepares him for his eventual place in domestic life. Puppies removed from the litter at this point often make poor pets, as they cannot adequately relate to other dogs or humans; they are either too nervous or overly aggressive. At this stage the puppy learns how to get around, taking on such challenges as stairs and thick carpets inside the house or tall grass and paved walkways outside.

From eight to ten weeks of age the puppy is fully weaned from his mother. He needs exposure to plenty of new locations and stimuli at this point, and the more positive human contact he can receive, the better. The puppy learns to want the company of people, not just of his mother and littermates. Simple training, such as teaching him his name or how to walk on a leash, can begin at this time. The puppy also should be allowed to explore his surroundings. Training at this age should be fun, not formal and not stressed. Inquisitive, active puppies can get themselves into dangerous situations, so the puppy must be supervised at this age. If not, he may chew electric cords or injure himself in rambunctious play.

At eleven to twelve weeks of age the puppy is well socialized and ready for his new home. While separation from his littermates will be traumatic, the excitement of a new life will quickly entice him and win him over. At this point the puppy goes on to develop his own personality, and simple obedience and housebreaking training can begin.

SELECTING YOUR PUPPY

Before you begin the search for that special puppy to share your home, there are several issues that you must first resolve. The most important question of all is whether or not you are ready to commit yourself to being a responsible dog owner. Is there time in your life to devote to your new companion, or will he be left alone for long stretches of time while you are at work or school? Are *all* members of your family happy about getting a puppy or do some view him as an intrusion? Questions such as these must be honestly answered before you make the decision to get a puppy, as this is a long-term commitment and you must do what is best for both you and the animal.

Young Cara Goodwin **(top)** has found a prickly friend. Remember that children must be taught how to properly pick up and handle their pet dogs; otherwise, both parties are liable to get hurt. The handling of Shar-peis requires extra care, since their coats are rather harsh to the touch. Wong Tsai, a two-month-old male bred by J. P. Chan of Cho Sun Kennel, Hong Kong **(bottom)**.

"Petunia" quickly learns to play ball **(top).** Shar-peis have much to offer as family pets: they are intelligent, clean, easily housebroken, and great watchdogs. Most people find Shar-pei puppies irresistible, as is the case with Kathy and this three-week-old pup **(bottom).** Look at those nice wide-open eyes.

MALE OR FEMALE?

While dogs of both sexes make good pets, there are a few differences that you may want to consider. If you are interested in breeding and raising a litter of puppies, you should, of course, select a good-quality female (a bitch). Those who do not plan on breeding their dogs should bear in mind that a nonneutered female will attract males whenever she comes into heat. These heat cycles occur approximately every six months, last two to three weeks, and can be very annoying. Spaying will eliminate this problem. Females are generally regarded as a little more gentle than males, and, therefore, have been acclaimed as better housepets.

Males are often slightly larger than their female counterparts, with a higher activity level and a stronger tendency to roam. While both sexes are equally loving and loyal, females have been touted as superior watchdogs because they are less likely to be distracted by outside forces. Males, however, are noted for being more aggressive against intruders.

WHAT AGE IS BEST?

While puppies certainly are the most adorable at six weeks of age, this is not the most advantageous age from an owner's point of view. At six weeks the puppy is like a baby that requires care twenty-four hours a day. He is too young to reliably housebreak, he requires four or more feedings a day, and he is undisciplined. In fact, a much higher percentage of four- to-six-week-old puppies die shortly after being placed with new owners than do eight-week-olds who have greater stamina. From an economic standpoint, it is certainly best for breeders or pet shops to sell their puppies when they are very young; they do not incur the additional expense of those first few trips to the veterinarian. But from a buyer's standpoint, one must consider how much time one has to devote to a puppy's early care before setting out to purchase that new family member.

Purchase your puppy when you find the one you feel will be best for you—whether he is six weeks old or six months old. One possible solution for dealing with primary puppy care is to board the six-week-old puppy with the breeder for a month or two after you purchase him. Experienced breeders are generally more adept at dealing with the needs of puppies and may be amenable to this arrangement for a fee, of course. If you are considering the purchase of an adult dog that has never been kept as a housepet, be sure to check his disposition carefully, as he may have trouble adjusting to family life.

SHOW QUALITY OR PET QUALITY?

When purchasing your purebred puppy, you must decide whether you want him to be a companion or whether you want to show him in competition. This is very important because only the finest breed specimens should be entered into active competition. Show-quality puppies are the hardest to find and are the most expensive to buy. If you are not interested in dog-show exhibiting, any healthy, well-bred specimen of the breed should do.

If showing is your intention, you should buy a puppy from a knowledgeable and reputable breeder. The puppies available in pet shops or from most neighborhood owners are generally termed "pet quality." This does not mean that they will make inferior or superior pets as compared to show-quality dogs; it just means that they are somehow slightly faulty when measured against the breed's standard of perfection. This faultiness is rarely evident to anyone except a breeder or dog-show judge and is of great concern only when you are entering the dog in competition. Be sure to make your desire to show the dog clear to the breeder so that he or she will sell you the best specimen possible that you can afford. Dedicated breeders strive to produce the finest dogs they can, ones that will enhance the quality of the breed. Not all dogs owned by even the top breeders are of superior quality when compared against the standard; therefore, a breeder may stipulate that you may not breed the pet-quality animal and thereby pass on his faulty traits. So bear this in mind and be sure to clarify your breeding intentions at the time of sale. Also, be aware that you will pay top prices for show dogs and for those females with brood bitch potential.

ONE DOG OR MORE?

Dogs, once they mature from puppyhood, generally prefer the attention of humans to the companionship of another dog, so there is no real need to buy your puppy a companion unless he is to be

This goes on all the time—Red makes kissing noises and W. J. (Fingertail Wu Jo) is right there **(top)**. Jim Deppen **(bottom)** with his two pals, Ch. Show Me E. F. Hutton Fingertail and Tai Seng Fingertail Fudge. The Fingertail dogs were bred by Jo Ann Webster, Raritan, New Jersey.

No matter what the sex, male or female, a Shar-pei is a wonderful companion and a loving family pet. This toddler **(top)** seems to be enjoying the company of her seven-week-old fawn male puppy. Bred by Jo Ann Webster of Fingertail Kennel. It's usually love at first sight for anyone seeing Shar-pei puppies for the first time, as it was for Kathy Weathers with this frisky litter **(bottom).** The abundance of wrinkling and the woebegone faces really touch the heart.

204

left alone a lot of the time. If this is the case, the second dog may help counteract loneliness, but you run the risk of having two unhappy pets on your hands.

If you are introducing a puppy into a home with an older dog, remember that there will be a period of adjustment for both dogs. The older dog may manifest signs of jealousy and resent the intrusion of the puppy. To counteract this, be sure to give the older dog lots of attention. At feeding time be sure to watch both dogs—especially the puppy, who, not knowing the rules, may try to steal from the other dog's bowl. Most adult dogs will accept a new dog in the home after a day or two; but if either dog shows any aggressiveness, you may want to keep them separated. Introduce them to each other for short periods of time until they become more accustomed to each other.

PURCHASING YOUR PUPPY

Once you've decided that you are ready to commit yourself to being a good owner and you've selected those characteristics and traits that you want in your dog, where do you go to locate that specific puppy you've been thinking so much about? You have several options.

If a pet-quality puppy is what you have in mind, start with your local newspaper and see if there are any ads for locally-bred litters. You can also obtain pet-quality puppies from established kennels who generally price their dogs according to their show potential. While you may pay more for a puppy from a professional breeder than you would from a local mating, you may be able to see several generations of your dog's ancestors at the breeder's kennel. This should give you a good indication of what your puppy will look and act like when it grows up. Make sure you see both or at least one of the puppy's parents.

In the case of a show-quality puppy, it is best if you visit more than one breeder and evaluate as many litters as you can find, even if you think you've found the right dog. You should be able to locate several breeders in your area by consulting the ads in newspapers and the various publications distributed by dog clubs. If you are looking for a true top-quality specimen, you should attend some dog shows and talk to the exhibitors. Some may have puppies or young dogs for sale or know of some people who do.

At the very least, these breed enthusiasts can acquaint you with the finer points of what to look for and give you inside information on how to proceed, where to go, and what to pay.

SIGNS OF GOOD HEALTH

When evaluating litters of puppies in an attempt to select the one that is right for you, what should you look for? Your primary concern should be for signs of good health. A puppy should look plump and well-fed. His ribs and hip bones should not be protruding prominently. A very thin or potbellied puppy may have worms and should be carefully inspected by a veterinarian. A healthy puppy should have clear eyes and there should be no discharge from his eyes or nose. The coat should be filling in nicely, without bare patches or obvious sores, and there should be no sign of a rash on the inside of the dog's legs or on his abdomen. Check his hearing ability by standing behind the puppy and making loud noises. He should quickly respond to the commotion and turn to you. Given that most puppies you see will pass this basic health exam, what else should you be looking for?

Among a litter of healthy puppies, one may stand out as the most jovial or outgoing. He may do things to attract your attention and generally seem to like you, as if he has picked *you* for his own! Be sure he is vigorous and of similar size with his littermates. Generally the runt or giant of the litter does not grow into the best specimen. He should be alert and full of energy, not listless and shy. A puppy's feet and bones will look out of proportion with his size. Don't worry, he will eventually balance out. Concern yourself with his general appearance and that of the area he has been raised in. A caring, thoughtful breeder will not allow his breeding quarters and animals to become infested with parasites, and such good breeding care often results in healthy, lively dogs.

Once you have selected your puppy, arrange with the owner to allow the dog to be taken to your veterinarian for a health examination. Most breeders or pet shops will let you return the dog within a few days if he should fail the health exam for any reason. Get this in writing, and be sure of the terms. Some owners will replace the ailing dog with another dog and some will return all your money. This agreement, however, generally does not apply if you have a change of heart; it applies only if the dog is certified, by the vet, as being physically unfit.

Before you take the puppy home, be sure to ask the breeder for all of the puppy's inoculation and health records. The breeder also may be able to familiarize you with some of your puppy's habits or personality traits. Did he have a favorite toy or blanket that you could take home with you to help ease the transition to his new home? Ask what and how often the puppy has been fed. Try not to vary this diet very much once you have gotten him home, to avoid possible stomach or bowel upset. Some thoughtful breeders often give the new owners a few days' supply of the puppy's food so that he can continue eating the same food in his new environment.

PAPERS

At the time of sale, arrange with the breeder to furnish you with your purebred puppy's registration papers from the national kennel club. Depending on the age of the dog, you may be given the registration application or the completed registration certificate, if this has already been received back from the registering body. Once a litter is born, the breeder generally applies to register the litter, specifying the names of the sire and dam and stating the number of puppies. The governing kennel club then issues a registration application for each of the qualifying puppies. If you are purchasing a six-to-ten-week-old puppy, this application will most likely be what you receive. With this, you will give the dog his official name and transfer ownership of the puppy from the breeder to you. The breeder will have to supply some of the information on the form, so discuss this application procedure with him or her if you are not sure how to proceed.

If you are purchasing a slightly older dog, he may have been registered with the national kennel club and a registration certificate may have already been issued. In this case you will need to write to the national club to arrange a transfer of ownership. If transfer forms are not available from the breeder, such forms can be obtained by writing to:

The American Kennel Club
51 Madison Avenue
New York, New York, 10010

The Kennel Club of Great Britain
1 Charges Street
Piccadilly, London, W1, England

The Canadian Kennel Club
111 Eglinton Avenue East
Toronto, Ontario M6S 4V7

The Australian Kennel Club
Royal Show Grounds
Ascot Vale, Victoria, Australia

Occasionally a breeder may purposely withhold the puppy's registration certificate from the new owner. This is generally done because the dog has a fault that is disqualifying, according to the breed or dog-show standards. This does not mean that the dog will not make a good pet, rather that the breeder is striving to eliminate the disqualifying traits from his dogs' future offspring. He may stipulate that the only way he will sell such a pet- quality animal is if the new owner agrees not to breed him. Once the puppy has been neutered, the breeder usually will render the registration material, should the owner still want the dog registered. Through the actions of such conscientious breeders, the overall quality of purebred dogs is enhanced for future generations.

THE FIRST DAY HOME
Hopefully you have already prepared an area of your home for the new arrival and stocked up on the items you and he will need in the early weeks:

> puppy food
> food and water bowls
> brush and comb
> bed or sleeping box
> collar and leash (or a one-piece
> lead)

The first day in a new home is going to be traumatic for your puppy, and very young puppies can be particularly unnerved. Try to make the transition easy for him by letting him get acquainted with the new environment on his own. Continuous play and attention will quickly overtire him. While it may take a lot of willpower on your part, try to keep the attention you give him to a minimum. Show him to his quarters, supplying him with some water and a little food, and leave the rest up to him. After a little rest, the puppy may be better prepared to meet all the members of his new family. A cautious introduction such as this will not overwhelm the puppy and will make him eager, not fearful, to learn more about his new surroundings.

Be sure in the first meeting that all family members, especially children, know the proper method of handling and picking up a puppy. You should place one hand under his hindquarters and the other across the chest. Never pick him up by the paws or legs or by the back of the neck. This could damage the still immature muscles and ligaments.

While you should start housebreaking lessons the first day, don't be too stern or expect the puppy to really understand what's expected of him. Mistakes are bound to happen, so confine the puppy to a small area. Provide him with a sleeping box or a bed for his naps, and try to comfort and reassure him if he starts to cry. The puppy should be kept indoors until he has received his first round of immunizations.

THE PUPPY BED OR SLEEPING BOX

Whether you intend to let your dog sleep in the house or whether you will eventually supply him with a dog house in the yard, it is advisable to keep him indoors until he is about six months old—especially during cold periods of the year. The puppy bed is not only an effective tool in easing his transition from the security of his mother and littermates to your home, but it will also aid in the housebreaking process. Dogs are born with a natural instinct for keeping their sleeping quarters clean; so, given a choice, they will look elsewhere for a spot to relieve themselves.

A box is best for the four-to-eight-week-old puppy. You should hold off buying a bed until he is older and closer to his adult size. When choosing a spot for the bed, always place it in a warm, dry area that is free from drafts.

The puppy's box should be only slightly larger than he is. It should allow him to stand, turn around, and lie down at full length. He should not be able to make a mess in one end and lay comfortably in another. You can make an inexpensive sleeping box from a standard cardboard box. Never use a cardboard box that has previously been used to store fresh fruits or vegetables, as it may have been sprayed with pesticides to prevent spoilage. This residue could be harmful to young puppies.

Be sure to place plenty of ventilation holes in the sides of the box and line the bottom of the box with several layers of newspaper, which is easily disposable. Unless the room the box is kept in is on the chilly side, hold off putting a blanket in the box for a week or two, as the puppy tends to push the blanket into one corner and is then uncomfortable trying to sleep on it. You should also make a lid to cover the box at night. Without the lid, the puppy will continuously try to climb out of the box. This only leads to his becoming anxious and crying.

During the first days in his new home when he is to be alone—which is a new experience for him, as he has always enjoyed the companionship of his littermates and mother—you can leave a radio playing softly nearby to help soothe him. At night, placing a loud ticking clock near the box will remind him of his mother and allow him to sleep more easily. You may also want to fill a hot water bottle with warm water, wrap it in a fluffy towel, and place this in his box as another comfort. These extraordinary measures should be necessary only for the first week or two, as the puppy will quickly adjust to his new home and routine.

The puppy *wants* to keep his bed clean, but he will be forced to relieve himself if he is not taken out at regular intervals. Expect a few accidents the first few days. The newspaper bedding should be changed daily whenever this happens. As the puppy grows, you may have to get a larger box; or he may do well with his early housebreaking lessons and then you can move him to his permanent bed.

While it is necessary for a new puppy to play with and be loved by his new family, a young puppy tires easily and needs many naps each day. Try to place him in his box for as many of these naps as possible to make him feel secure in the box. This will allow him to adjust to the box and it will help to keep him from crying at night.

Once the puppy settles into a housebreaking routine, it is a good time to consider buying him a permanent bed. Be sure to place the bed in an area that he likes or he may not use it. Some beds come with mattresses that contain scented materials, such as cedar. Many dogs do not like this smell and will not use the bed because of it. Other dogs just don't enjoy sleeping on a dog bed and often prefer a rug or a soft piece of furniture. Hopefully you and the dog can arrange a mutually agreeable spot for him to sleep. If he should choose a place where you do not want him, correct him each time he goes to it. He may soon lose interest in the desired location if it is unavailable to him.

Some owners prefer to supply their dog with a mat to lie on, placing it either directly on the floor or in a sleeping basket. While most dogs take readily to this, be careful to buy a mat of natural fiber. Mats that are dyed can cause an allergic reaction in some dogs, which can result in skin irritations and other disorders.

HOUSEBREAKING

No aspect of dog ownership warrants more concern among owners of puppies than housebreaking. Will my puppy learn quickly? What is the easiest, most efficient method? What is the puppy to do when I am not home to let him out?

The most important point to keep in mind is that dogs instinctively want to keep their sleeping quarters clean. This will aid greatly in the housebreaking process. However, you must remember that a puppy cannot be expected to be able to control his elimination reflexes at an early age. While he is very young, it is best to anticipate his needs. He will need to relieve himself at certain times each day: after waking, after each meal, late at night, and after any period of great excitement or vigorous exercise. Until he is reliably housebroken, make sure he is in the appropriate area at these important times. Praise him when he relieves himself in his assigned spot, even if you had to whisk him there at the very last second.

Serious housebreaking can begin at three months of age, but don't expect perfection at first. A realistic goal for a dog that is completely housebroken is six months. Until then, a few "accidents" are bound to occur.

The most efficient method of housebreaking is to train the puppy directly to the outdoors; but this requires your being available to take him out whenever the need arises, as a puppy cannot be expected to wait for any length of time. The more practical, although an untidy and prolonged method, is to first paper train the puppy and then eventually break him to going outdoors.

Assign an area several feet square near the door as the temporary spot for the newspapers. The puppy should be kept confined to this room when not under direct supervision in another area of the house. Begin the paper training the first day by making use of the first "accident" you find. Soak a piece of newspaper in the

A handful of three-week-old pups belonging to Bedlam Kennels **(top).** An eight-week-old puppy **(bottom)** named "Bullet," owned by the Wangs of Lexington, Kentucky. Contrary to popular belief, Shar-pei puppies *do not* housebreak themselves. They do have a natural instinct for cleanliness; however, they will need some assistance from you.

212

puppy's urine. Save this piece and place it on the clean newspapers to serve as a scent marker for the proper area. You should have to do this only once or twice before the puppy knows where he is permitted to relieve himself.

Be sure to thoroughly clean the site of all accidents, especially carpets. If any odor is allowed to remain, the dog will recognize the scent and return to repeat his misdeed. Rinse the area with soapy water, to which a little vinegar or ammonia has been added, to overpower the smell of urine. Remove all excess water and allow the area to dry.

Always be on the lookout in the early days for signs that your pup needs to relieve himself. He may whimper or cry, look restless, sniff the floor, or run anxiously around the room. At this point you should place him on the newspapers and praise him when he uses the area. As he becomes accustomed to this process and uses the papers reliably, reduce the size of the papers.

You will probably want to eliminate the papers as soon as it is possible for the puppy to go outside when he needs to. If he is to be left alone all day while you are at work or school, however, this will take some time, as puppies cannot be expected to have complete control of their elimination reflexes until they are grown. If this is the case, keep the puppy confined to a small area covered with the newspapers while you are out.

It is important to prevent the puppy from becoming totally dependent on the newspapers. Some paper-trained dogs have been known to play outside for hours and scratch anxiously to get into the house to use the papers when the need arises. Encourage your dog to use the designated areas outside and soon he should adapt easily to relieving himself away from the papers. Begin outdoor housebreaking at a time of day when you know he will need to relieve himself, especially in the morning as soon as he has awakened. Take him out on his leash and walk him back and forth in a small area. Praise him when he goes. He may, however, be confused about what is expected of him. You may find it easier to place a small piece of paper on the ground. This will be necessary only once or twice, as the dog will quickly learn that it is permissible to use the area you have brought him to. Regardless of whether this area is on your property or in a public place, it is the owner's responsibility to clean up all solid wastes, not only as a

213

courtesy to everyone but also to help prevent potential health problems. "Pooper scooper" laws are in effect in many cities and towns, and failure to clean up after your dog may result in a hefty fine.

In general, a female puppy usually requires a shorter outdoor walk to accomplish her elimination mission, while a male may opt for a longer walk with more stops. He is more concerned with marking his territory. As puppies, both sexes will squat. A male dog will begin to lift his leg when he is nearly grown.

The housebreaking process should not be too drawn out if you give the dog the proper amount of attention, encouragement, and praise. Have patience and do not rush him along. Remember: *accidents do happen*. If you catch him in the act in a forbidden area, give a forceful "No!" and show him the proper area. NEVER rub his nose in his excreta. This is a degrading action that accomplishes nothing except to make him fearful and more confused. He should never be hit (even with a rolled-up newspaper), yelled at, or chased in response to a mistake, and food should never be withheld as a punishment. Correct inappropriate behavior with firm but loving guidance and make clear what the appropriate behavior should be. Praise all accomplishments.

Remember, dogs are naturally clean and want to keep their quarters clean. If you are experiencing a problem after several months of consistent training, the use of a dog crate may help eliminate the problem. When you are not available to supervise the dog, confine him to this crate. Placing a dog in a proper dog crate is not a form of punishment. Most dogs, if introduced to the crate while young, react favorably to the crate and find it comforting—it is a spot of their own. Unless your dog is ill, he will try his best not to soil the crate. However, he will still have to be taken out of the crate at regular intervals to relieve himself. The crate is a temporary aid, not a jail. He should be given plenty of time outside of it. When you think he needs relief, show him to the proper location and praise him highly when he complies with what you expect of him. As he matures and learns to control his reflexes, you will be able to remove the crate and leave the dog alone, as long as regularly scheduled elimination intervals are maintained. No dog can be expected to endure more than eight to ten hours without relieving himself. If you cannot be available at

Training should begin when a dog is young so that good habits are formed early in life. It is important to establish rules of the house, to be consistent in the enforcement of those rules, and to lavish the dog with praise as a reward for a job well done.

regular intervals, you must either resign yourself to having a perpetually paper-trained dog or postpone dog ownership until a time when you can supply more attention to the animal.

If you are lucky enough to have easy access to the outdoors, you may wish to install a small flexible door for your dog to give him instant entry to the yard. Once in the yard be sure he actually tends to his business and does not forget the purpose of his trip out. There are plenty of distractions that can entice an eager puppy. Most dogs appreciate the freedom such a swinging door affords, but owners must properly secure the area to which a dog has access by fencing in the yard or constructing a dog run.

Bedlam Kennels' Sis Q's Chin-Ho learning the "sit." Owner, Ellen Weathers Debo.

Chapter 10

Basic Obedience Training

Discipline is a key component of the pet/owner relationship—as vital as supplying the dog with the proper amount of love and care. Obedience training ensures a happy future for all concerned, as the dog is taught the manners he will need to participate in family life.

From an early age a dog needs to know who is in charge and what is right and wrong, or he will continually test his owner. By nature, dogs think they are the boss unless there is another more dominant force in the picture. At birth, for example, the dog's mother is the boss. You must earn your position as boss by teaching your pet that only appropriate behavior will be tolerated and that you will not accept his testing of your authority. This is not accomplished by making the dog live in fear of your wrath, but by teaching him what is expected of him and being consistent and fair in the enforcement of these guidelines. Once this is settled you can look forward to owning a pet who can be relied upon to be responsible in the home and in public.

Most dogs are adept at learning and therefore thrive on it. The best way to work with this natural inclination towards learning is to begin by teaching some very simple, easily accomplished tasks and progress very slowly to more complicated skills as the dog proves he understands and remembers what he has been taught. Even if you have never trained a dog before, with a little patience and effort you should be able to teach any dog such basic commands as Sit, Stay, and Come. If you exhibit a flair for training and your dog is a good learner you may want to proceed with more advanced training skills, but at the very least he will require both a basic working knowledge of how to act in common situations and the ability to be controlled.

Some common-sense rules should apply in training your dog. First of all, if you begin training with a young puppy and find that he is very confused, he may be too young to give you the concentration that is required and you would do best to postpone the lessons for a few weeks until he is older and better prepared. A puppy should be allowed some freedom while he is young, and you should not expect true obedience at an early age. If you work him too hard when he is young, you may break his spirit and be left with a fearful or overly passive adult dog. You want to begin *formal* skills training when you think the dog really understands what you want, generally around six or eight months of age, although you should certainly try to teach him your rules of right and wrong as soon as he comes to live with you.

There are a few basic rules you should follow during every training lesson. Keep the lessons fairly short and to the point, usually ten minutes in the beginning. This will enable the dog to retain his concentration and eagerness to learn. Do not let things get too unstructured so that training seems like all fun and games. Obedience is serious business and you should make the dog aware of this. You should be firm but not scolding, and be quick to praise the dog when he has done well. You should not, of course, praise him so highly that he gets overexcited and forgets all he has learned.

Consistency is a key aspect of training. You should hold your lessons regularly, not in a hit-or-miss fashion. Use the same commands each time you work on a certain skill, not Sit one time and Sit Down the next. It is also effective if you call the dog by his name before each request, such as "Sam, Sit." You should always require a consistent response from the dog; never accept a partial completion of any command.

You must be patient and be prepared for many repetitions of the desired behavior until it is learned by your dog. There is no room for anger. When you speak to the dog, use a firm, authoritative tone of voice. Do not shout at him, no matter how frustrated you may get. Such behavior will only confuse him and make things worse. Never nag at him. When you speak to him during training, mean it and be clear as to what you expect him to do. When he responds incorrectly, correct him appropriately and repeat the exercise. Correction should be made in such a way as to inspire him to do better. With each slight improvement or correct response, reward him with petting and kind words.

During the early phases of training the dog will not understand how he is expected to respond. He will learn through making errors and receiving guidance from you. Correct lovingly, not angrily. There is a definite distinction between correction and punishment. Punishment should be reserved as a response to *willful misbehavior only*. Confusion in the dog requires patient correction, not punishment from a tired, frustrated owner. Never punish a dog if you are in doubt about his intent. Constant punishment can ruin the training process, so be sure not to ask the dog to give too much during the early lessons. If you find you cannot calmly continue to supply the dog with fair correction, stop for the day and give it another try when you are well rested and at ease. Some people have great difficulty with this, and if this is the case you may want to consider hiring an experienced trainer to take over, or perhaps another family member may have better success.

To facilitate concentration for both owner and dog, plan the lessons for a time of day when hunger and tiredness do not come into play. In the summer, train in the cool of the early morning or evening; the lessons should take place in a location that has few distractions, one that is well ventilated.

One very important rule: Always end your lessons on a positive note. If things are going well, do not get carried away and continuously push the dog to do "just one more" exercise or repetition. Praise the dog for his good work and quit for the day. Working the dog beyond the limits of his concentration will result in confusion and will set back the training process.

If things are not going well, try to reassure the dog and have him perform some very simple task that he is already familiar with to end the lesson. Praise him and let him know you appreciate the effort he is making. The next lesson hopefully will be more successful.

If you end a lesson abruptly, on a negative note, the dog will not want to participate again. He will fear displeasing you and become more of a problem with each failure. Proceed very slowly and praise each new accomplishment, no matter how small. Moving very slowly in the initial stages of training may seem tedious to you but it will pay off in the end as your dog learns how to learn. The ultimate goal is to have the dog come to enjoy and thrive on the training process, not fear it.

At the end of every lesson let your dog do something that he enjoys, such as romp in the yard or play a game of chase with you. Ending the lessons pleasantly will keep him interested and he will associate training with pleasing you and having fun. And pleasing you, pleases him.

THE EARLY LESSONS

The first lesson to teach your dog is to recognize his name. During the time you have owned your dog you have, hopefully, been calling him by one name. A short name is easiest for the dog to learn. Even the show dog with a long string of names should be called by one simple name at home. If you use his name frequently, a puppy will quickly learn to recognize it. When he responds as you call him, reward him with praise or a tidbit.

Whether or not to use food bits as rewards for proper behavior is a matter for you to consider. In the beginning training sessions, this will encourage the dog to respond to your commands, but the aim of training is to teach the dog proper behavior—not how to respond in order to receive a reward. It is best to keep such rewards infrequent and eliminate them altogether once the dog's natural keenness to learn is aroused. If the dog is consistently rewarded in this manner you will never be quite sure whether he is responding because he has learned the command or whether he wants the tidbit. Some dogs may hurry through an exercise, giving a sloppy performance, just for the anticipated reward. This, of course, is unsatisfactory.

Once your dog begins to respond routinely to his commands, never allow him to respond sloppily. He must fully perform the requested behavior as he was taught. Bright dogs tend to test their masters now and then, just to see how much they can get away with. You will earn his respect by being firm and consistent with him. However, when correction is called for do not go too far and physically hurt or humiliate the dog. Such behavior is destructive not only to the learning process but also to the entire pet/owner relationship.

Another simple skill to teach the puppy is to follow you. This will not only bond the two of you as partners but will get him to really enjoy your company. Begin by following *him* wherever he goes, treating this as a game. As soon as he starts to move toward you, entice him into following you around the house. Frequently stop and start to keep things interesting. This simple skill will later aid in teaching the dog to walk easily on a leash and to heel at your side.

TRAINING TO LEAD

The leash is a fundamental tool in the training process. One of the first things you must do is let your dog become familiar with his collar and leash. Choose a collar that fits—not one he will grow into. Slip it over his neck and pet him reassuringly. When he has gotten used to it, tie a short piece of rope or cloth to the collar to let him feel the slight tug of an attachment to the collar. If this goes well, remove the rope or cloth and attach a lightweight leash. At first, let him drag it around. Carefully monitor him, though, so that he does not get caught on anything.

Once he is not bothered by the presence of the leash, pick it up and loosely hold it. Try your familiar follow-the-leader game and see if he is bothered by the leash's weight. Getting him to move around in this manner should keep him from fearing the use of the leash and prepare him for the next stages, where pressure is applied and the leash becomes a tool of restraint.

The next step is to tie him for a short period. Choose a spot with which he is familiar and comfortable. Make sure there are not items he can tangle with and choke himself on. Leave him alone for a short time, several times a day. At first he may whine and try to break away. If he gets unruly, calm him but do not release him. After several unsuccessful attempts at getting away, he will learn that the leash means he is no longer free to do as he pleases. At this point it becomes a training aid. Be sure to check the dog periodically, not only to verify his safety but to make sure he is not chewing on the leash. The leash is not a toy, it is a tool and a symbol of authority. If he should try to put the leash in his mouth, tell him "No" and mean it. If he persists, a slight upward tug will remove the leash from his mouth. You may want to consider using a light but sturdy metal leash until he no longer entertains the notion of chewing to rid himself of the leash.

The first few experiences at being tied should be kept very short, then very gradually increase the time he is tethered. Be sure to praise him for his good behavior each time you release him. You want him to adjust to this temporary constraint, not come to resent it.

Once he does not balk at your attaching the leash, you are ready to attempt a short walk on lead. Call him to your side, attach the leash to his collar, and move off. If he will not move, or if he pulls against the lead, continue to move and pull him along as best you can. Of course, do not allow him to hurt himself. If he lunges forward, straining the leash to get away, try to entice him back to your side or just hold him back as best you can. By continually applying pressure to his neck, he will have no choice but to learn that it is useless to struggle and that it is much more comfortable to walk than be pulled! Do not jerk him along, as this could injure his neck. When he gives up the struggle, reward him. Should he appear afraid, reassure him with praise and petting. Keep the first walks short and preferably in familiar terrain. Talk to him as you walk, in a low, friendly tone and pet him occasionally.

TRAINING TO SIT

This lesson should be taught indoors or in an area free from distractions (such as birds overhead, passing cars, children, etc.). The dog should be on lead and then he can be taught to sit in front of you or at your side. Place the leash in your right hand and hold it taut, with slight upward pressure. Give the command "Sit" and at the same time lean over with your left hand and press down on his rump until he is in the proper sitting position. Press steadily but not roughly. Once he is sitting, he may want to lie down or slide over on his side. Continue the upward pressure and straighten him up with your left hand. As soon as he is back in the proper position, praise him lavishly.

222

Hon. Ch. Jade East Lady St. Lucifer **(top)** and Hon. Ch. Jade East Oriental Mosaic **(bottom),** both by Tzo Tzo's Hei Te Ying out of Reddy's Black Gem O'Bedlam. Loretta Anders, Greenville, South Carolina, owner.

223

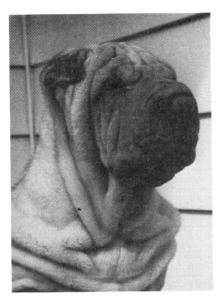 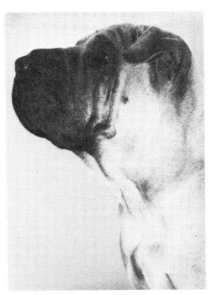

Loong Ch'ai Ho-Ghee Poon, a six-month-old Ro Ro II grandson **(top, left)**. Owner, Betsy Davison, Sarasota, Florida. A Shir Du Sam Ku granddaughter, Sui Yeen's Loong Nu, in 1981 **(top, right)**. Bred by Rose Stone and owned by Betsy Davison. Sui Yeen's Lu Chen **(bottom)**.

In the early lessons do not make him stay in the sit position for too long. Release the pressure from the leash and let him walk around a bit. After a minute or two, repeat the entire procedure. Use the same commands and actions, as this will help him understand what you are asking him to do. Be sure to reward him when he reaches the proper sit position, not when he breaks to get up. When he tries to break, tell him "No, Sit" and reposition him. Be clear, as he must learn to associate the reward with the sitting action.

Repeat the Sit lesson several times a day, but keep the initial lessons short and do not attempt more than five or six sits. As he progresses, exert less and less pressure on his rump each time. Eventually he will associate the command with the pressure, whether you actually apply it or not, and he will drop into the proper position at the sound of the command. Once this occurs, you can try to have him remain in the position for more than a few seconds, but not until he becomes distracted. When he stays for these short instances, praise him with "Good dog" and some petting. This is the first step in teaching him the Stay.

TRAINING TO STAY

Once your dog is responding perfectly to the Sit, place him in this position but retain a slight pressure from the lead on his neck. Gradually back away from him, only a foot or so at first; this time command him to "Stay." As you begin to move, simultaneously swing your hand forward toward his face, with the palm and fingers pointing down. Stop short of touching his nose. This hand signal should always be done at the instant you command him to stay and begin to move away from him.

Upon seeing you move, your dog will probably try to move toward you or to lie down. As soon as he breaks the position, return him to the Sit in the original location and repeat the entire Stay command. Be patient. While this lesson should be learned pretty easily, it is natural for the dog to be confused at first. Have the dog stay for a few seconds at first and increase the time gradually. At the end of each Stay, praise him profusely for a job well done.

It will take many repetitions for you to reliably expect your dog to stay for any length of time. Continue to drill him daily and you will eventually be able to have him remain still for up to thirty minutes, even with you out of sight.

TRAINING TO COME

Once your puppy knows his name, there should be little difficulty in getting him to come when called. As a puppy, he may be slow to respond, since a myriad of things may have his attention. The importance of this command is to teach the dog that he *must* respond when called, at once, regardless of where he is or what he is doing. The Come can be a life-saving command when used to extricate the dog from a dangerous situation.

You will need a large area for practicing this command and a light check cord of approximately twenty feet. Attach the cord to his collar and let him move about in the area. When you see that he is occupied with something, call him by name and command him to "Come." If he responds, praise him, and let him return to his romp. Repeat the command at various intervals. Most likely, he will tire of being interrupted and sooner or later will not respond. At this point, grasp the check cord, repeat the Come command, and give him a jerk. If he still does not respond properly, repeat the command and jerk several times. Generally, this should be enough to get your point across; but if all fails, repeat the command and reel him in. Reward him when he arrives. After one or two more successful commands, end the lesson and let him enjoy some freedom.

This command can be repeated several times a day, but do not overdo it. Three or four comes per lesson are plenty. If you push him too far he may not leave your side after being called, since he feels he is just going to be called back as soon as he leaves. This is disheartening to the dog. The object is to make him come when he is needed, not to make him behave like a robot.

Under no circumstances should you ever punish the dog when he comes to you. If you catch him in a punishable act, *go to him* and correct him. Do not call him to you and then lower the boom. This will make him wary of answering the Come.

As your dog progresses in his obedience training, he may become proficient at performing without the leash. You should never attempt off-leash work until you are certain that he can be trusted implicitly, and even then you should always begin this work in a confined area, such as a fenced yard. As previously mentioned, many dogs like to test their owners from time to time to see what they can get away with, and having him pull such a trick in an open area could be disastrous. With patience and a lot of work, you can eventually teach your dog to work off the leash and to respond to a whistle or hand signals—it all depends on how much time and effort you wish to put into the training process.

TRAINING TO DOWN

Like the Come, the Down can be a life-saving command if the dog gets himself into trouble. However, it is generally used when you just want to keep the dog in check.

After he has mastered the Sit, the Down should not be hard to teach. Place him in the sit position, and as you command him to "Down" use your right hand to pull his front feet out from under him and thereby cause him to slide down. Another method is to place the leash under your foot, making it taut. Press on his shoulders as you give the command. You want him to be on all fours, not spread out and relaxed; so, put him into the proper position if he should get too comfortable.

Ultimately you want to release him from the Down with an upward movement of the hand. At first you may call "Up" with a wave of the hand to startle him into movement. The Down, as well as the Sit, can be used with the Stay to keep the dog restrained for a length of time up to thirty minutes. Many owners and trainers feel that it is good discipline training if you practice a long Down Stay each day. This will be a valuable aid when you need a length of time where you know the dog is under constraint and not under foot.

TRAINING TO HEEL

Even if advanced obedience training is not one's goal, everyone wants his dog to walk nicely at his side when out for a stroll. This is known as the Heel. The dog should always be positioned to walk on your left side with his chest in line approximately with your knee. The reason for placing the dog on your left is because you thus maintain the most control, positioning yourself between the dog and any possible danger.

Hold the leash in your right hand at first and use the left hand to apply pressure on the leash and thereby control the dog's speed. Give the command "Heel" and walk at your regular pace. Try to keep him in line, applying a tug if he lags behind. Should he try

227

to run ahead of you, first try a jerk of the leash to slow him down and return to the proper position. If this does not work and he continues to surge ahead, stop and place him in a Sit. Once he is patiently waiting, move out again, commanding him to "Heel" as he is released from the Sit. This stop-and-start process should get the point across to him very quickly that he is to move next to you, not out front or behind.

Keep the first lessons short, no more than ten or fifteen minutes. Any longer and he may grow tired or disinterested in going out for such excursions, especially if he is being placed in corrective sits.

TEACHING GOOD MANNERS

Aside from knowing the basic commands, your dog must be taught to control himself in all social situations. While no one wants a dog who acts like a shrinking violet or an overtrained robot, everyone wants a friendly companion who can be trusted to be on his good behavior, regardless of the situation and with little prodding from his owner.

Jumping Up. The overly exuberant dog greets all visitors or returning members of the household with a heartfelt welcome that includes his trying to jump into their arms. This practice should be discouraged when the tendency first begins to manifest itself, and there are several methods of correction.

The first method is to make the dog uncomfortable when he jumps up by holding on to his paws and making him remain with his two front legs in the air. Hold firmly but not so tightly as to cause the dog pain. You just want to frustrate him to the point where he can think of nothing else but getting his paws back on the ground. Speak to him, saying "No Jump" when you seize his paws. Repeat this procedure each time he jumps up and he will soon tire of the habit.

Another popular method is to raise your knee in response to his jumping, using it as a barrier that meets his chest and forces him back to the ground. While this is often successful, it can be harmful in that you can possibly injure the dog by applying too much force. Some dogs actually become more excited by the rejecting force of the knee and lunge forward even more vehemently in response. Used correctly, this method is a quick way to ward off the

228

jumping dog by placing a barrier that puts him off balance and gets him quickly back on the ground. Always couple the knee-to-the-chest motion with a "No Jump" command.

If all else fails, try the water pistol method. Keep a loaded water pistol near the dog and squirt him in the face each time he jumps up on someone entering your home, telling him "No Jump." The dog finds this most displeasing and may quickly discard the jumping habit.

Barking. While you do not want to rid the dog of barking altogether—as this is often good security protection for the household—you do not want a dog that barks uncontrollably out of loneliness, boredom, or in response to common noises such as the doorbell or telephone. When such noises occur, allow the dog a bark or two and then reprimand him, saying "No Bark" and jerk him on his collar. Through constant repetition of this formal correction you should be able to break the dog of the habit. If not, more dramatic measures are called for.

Squirt the dog in the face with water from a water pistol each time he barks incessantly, saying "No Bark." You must be sure to act swiftly, as he must associate the onset of barking with water in the face. Keep a water pistol loaded and in a handy location.

Some dogs can be broken of the barking habit by scolding and placing the dog in isolation, such as a small room. Others will learn quickly if they are met with a large splash of water in the face. Some, however, require drastic action. If this is the case, an electric shock collar can be purchased to quickly break the habit, but this should be used only in extreme cases and for a very limited time by people who know what they're doing.

Always investigate the source of your dog's barking before you give him the command to stop barking. A dog's ears are very sensitive and he may be responding to a situation that you are not aware of. Barking should be discouraged only when the dog does it to excess or for no constructive purpose.

Chasing Cars. The habit of chasing cars is often fatal to dogs so prone, and it puts motorists in jeopardy as well, as they can lose control of their automobiles in attempting to deal with the dog. Chasing cars is a habit best broken by not allowing the dog to roam free, but some dogs even try to take off after the cars while on leash or chained in the yard.

Shir Du puppies at six weeks old **(top)**—a real handful! *Never* pick up a puppy by its front legs, its ears, or the scruff of the neck. Hold the pup gently but firmly around the middle section and support its rear end so that it feels secure. Shir Du Clyde at one year **(bottom).** The Shir Du dogs were bred by Shirley and Dugan Skinner of Wolcottville, Indiana.

230

Matgo Law's homebred, Down-Homes Von Anne IV, pictured at four months. In 1979 she won Best of Breed and Group I from the puppy classes under USA judge R. G. Beauchamp.

If the dog attempts to chase a car while under restraint, react immediately to his attempts, sharply jerking him by the collar and saying "Stop" or "No!" You must then begin practice sessions to rid him of the habit. Walk him near the streets and await his lunges. Corrections must be very quick and very firm. You may want to set a trap for him by arranging with several friends to drive slowly past the dog. Should the dog attempt to go after the car, have the passenger-side occupant drop a bucket of water on his head. This should jolt him out of the desire to chase cars.

231

Hon. Ch. Linns Ping, C.D., the first Shar-pei to receive both championships. She also had the honor of appearing in a 1979 issue of *Life* magazine. Owners, Dick and Zell Llewellyn of Shoestring Acres Kennel, Alvin, Texas.

Chapter 11

Advanced Obedience Training and Competition

Once your dog has mastered the basic obedience commands and has shown that he is willing and eager to learn, you may want to consider advanced obedience training. The requirements for participation in obedience trials run by the American Kennel Club or other regulating organizations are quite demanding and a real commitment by both dog and handler is needed for success. Whether you train your dog on your own or join a professional training class, there will be many hours of practice required.

The American Kennel Club publishes a pamphlet that outlines the basic requirements for obedience trial competition. A copy of *Obedience Regulations* can be obtained by writing to the American Kennel Club at 51 Madison Avenue, New York, New York 10010.

Obedience trial competition differs greatly from show competition in that performance rather than conformation beauty is judged. In fact, dogs that are not eligible for show competition because of neutering or disqualifying physical faults can become obedience trial participants. The competitions can vary from the more informal match shows sponsored by local fanciers' clubs in which the dogs compete for ribbons and inexpensive trophies to the formal AKC-regulated trials sponsored by all-breed obedience clubs or held in conjunction with large conformation shows. Additionally, there are also competitions held for dogs skilled in tracking, whereby a dog competes in field trials where he is required to track a scent.

The AKC obedience trials are divided into three classes where dogs compete for degrees. The first class is Novice, with the title of C.D. (Companion Dog) being awarded after successful completion of the class requirements. The dog is then eligible to compete in the more difficult Open class for the title of C.D.X. (Companion Dog Excellent). Upon obtaining this degree, the dog moves on to the Utility class to compete for his U.D. (Utility Dog) title. The title of Obedience Trial Champion (O.T. Ch.) is awarded to U.D. title holders who receive a required number of first place finishes in advanced competition. A related obedience skill, although held in separate competition from the obedience trials, involves tracking. The T.D. (Tracking Dog) title is awarded in field competition for dogs that demonstrate the ability to recognize and follow human scent and to use this skill in the service of mankind.

To earn these degrees, the dog and handler must master the required exercises and perform them together to the satisfaction of the trial judges. The team is scored on a scale of 0 to 200 points, and they must receive at least 50% of the points for each exercise with a total score of at least 170 to earn a "leg" toward the degree. A dog must receive three "legs" under three separate judges at three obedience trials to achieve the degree.

The Novice class is open to any AKC-registered dog at least six months of age. The dog must perform the following exercises:

TEST	MAXIMUM SCORE
1. Heel on Leash and Figure Eight	40 Points
2. Stand for Examination	30 Points
3. Heel Free	40 Points
4. Recall	30 Points
5. Long Sit	30 Points
6. Long Down	30 Points
MAXIMUM TOTAL SCORE	200 Points

Upon receiving at least 50% of the points for each exercise, with a combined total of at least 170 at three trials under three different

234

Three-month-old Gold's Magic Moment, also known as "Maggie," in a serious pose **(top)** and a more relaxed pose **(bottom).** By Gold's Black Magic out of Tzo Tzo's 14 Karat Gold. Bred by Gayle and the late Marty Gold and owned by John and Betsy Davison, she is a Shir Du Sam Ku granddaughter.

judges, the letters C.D. can be used after the dog's name.

After earning the Companion Dog title, the dog can move on to Open class competition to vie for the title of Companion Dog Excellent. The Open competition will be divided into Open A class (for dogs that have won the C.D. title but not the C.D.X.) and Open B class (for dogs that have the C.D. or C.D.X. title). The following exercises must be performed:

TEST	MAXIMUM SCORE
1. Heel Free and Figure Eight	40 Points
2. Drop on Recall	30 Points
3. Retrieve on Flat	20 Points
4. Retrieve over High Jump	30 Points
5. Broad Jump	20 Points
6. Long Sit	30 Points
7. Long Down	30 Points
MAXIMUM TOTAL SCORE	200 Points

Upon receiving at least 50% of the points for each exercise, with a combined score of at least 170 at three trials under three different judges, the letters C.D.X. can be used after the dog's name.

After receiving the Companion Dog Excellent title, the dog can then attempt to earn the Utility Dog title. The Utility class competition may be divided into Utility A class (for dogs that have won the C.D.X. but not the U.D. title) and Utility B class (for U.D. title holders). To achieve this degree, the dog must receive at least 50% of the points in each exercise with a combined total of at least 170 at three trials under three different judges. He must perform these most difficult exercises:

TEST	MAXIMUM SCORE
1. Signal Exercise	40 Points
2. Scent Discrimination, Article No.1	30 Points
3. Scent Discrimination, Article No.2	30 Points
4. Directed Retrieve	30 Points
5. Directed Jumping	40 Points
6. Group Examination	30 Points
MAXIMUM TOTAL SCORE	200 Points

236

Dogs that have earned their Utility Dog title can compete for the title of Obedience Trial Champion by compiling a sufficient number of championship points. Championship points are awarded to those dogs that have earned a first or second place ribbon competing in Open B or Utility class (or Utility B, if divided) competition, according to a schedule of points established by the AKC. Requirements for this title are:

1. The dog shall have won 100 points.
2. The dog shall have won a first place in Utility (or Utility B, if divided) provided there are at least three dogs in competition.
3. The dog shall have won a first place in Open B provided there are at least six dogs in competition.
4. The dog shall have won a third first place under the conditions of 2 or 3 above.
5. The dog shall have won these three first places under three different judges.

Bedlam's Yo Ki Hi showing a good rear and sturdy bone—a well-balanced puppy, bred by the author.

Match shows offer good opportunity for puppies and handlers just starting out in their show careers. Here Oriental Treasure's Put n on the Ritz, a ten-month-old, is handled by Georgia Izzo for breeder/owner Maryann Smithers of Boonton, New Jersey.

Chapter 12

Showing Your Dog

As the owner of a purebred dog, you can be proud of your breed's heritage and breed qualities. But owning a purebred is no guarantee that he is a top-quality specimen as compared to the breed's standard of perfection. The dogs that win Best In Show honors are very rare indeed and are often the products of years of breeding efforts by knowledgeable breeders. Show- quality specimens are generally hard to find and will usually carry a hefty price tag if purchased from a breeder, although a few "Cinderella" champions can be found now and then from novice breeders. If you are looking for a potential show dog, familiarize yourself with the requirements of the breed standard and scrutinize as many litters as possible before selecting your dog.

While the dream of seeing one's perfectly groomed dog gait proudly around the show ring on his way to being named Best In Show at a major competition is attainable only by a select few pedigreed dog owners, participation in some aspect of the show game can be available to many owners.

TYPES OF DOG SHOWS

There are several types of dog shows that offer various levels of competition for purebred dogs. Fun matches are often sponsored by local dog clubs and fanciers to offer interested owners a chance to try their hand at showing their dogs. These are often small

239

shows with very modest entry fees that are collected at the door. The entered dogs may be judged in groups comprised of various breeds and both sexes. While various prizes and ribbons may be awarded, the real focus of this match show is to provide a fun time for all. Match shows give inexperienced handlers and their dogs a chance to gain ring poise and experience.

Sanctioned match shows are slightly more formal than fun matches, as they are run in accordance with the American Kennel Club guidelines. Your dog's success at a sanctioned match may be a good indicator of whether your dog may have a future in the show game. Although these matches offer no championship points, if your dog does well and places ahead of other entries of the same breed you might begin to seriously consider whether you want to take the next step up the show ladder—entering the championship shows.

Make the most of these match show experiences. As they are learning experiences, ask the judges for their opinion of your dog's chances and for an evaluation of your handling technique. Talk to the more experienced exhibitors for any tips or advice they may be able to give you. Not only beginners participate in match shows, as established kennels often enter their young dogs to acquaint the dogs with the show process. Match shows have much to offer aspiring competitors.

There are two types of shows where your dog can win points toward his championship title: all-breed shows and specialty shows. Specialty shows are limited to entries of one breed only, while all-breed shows are open to all AKC recognized breeds. An all-breed conformation show may be designated *benched* or *unbenched*. A benched show requires the dog to stay at his appointed bench area during the advertised hours of the show, although he may be removed to be taken to the exercise pen, to the grooming area (no more than one hour before his showing time), or to the appropriate judging area. The famous Westminster Kennel Club show is an example of a benched show. At an unbenched show the dog is only required to be present at the time of his judging. At such shows the dog can be kept in the owner's crate or car or any appropriate location, and he may leave as soon as his judging is completed.

Junior Showmanship is another aspect of the show game that is open to young handlers only. In this competition children between the ages of ten and seventeen handle dogs owned by their immediate families. Junior Showmanship provides children with the opportunity to experience the feel of the show ring and to train themselves for actual breed competition. In this activity the handling skills of the Junior Showmanship competitors are judged, not the conformation quality of the dog (although he must be a purebred). The children are separated by age and number of previous Junior Showmanship wins. The competitors are placed in divisions: Novice A for ten-to-twelve-year-olds who have not won three firsts in this class, Novice B for thirteen-to-sixteen-year-olds who have not won three firsts in this class, Open A for ten-to-twelve-year-olds who have won three firsts in Novice, and Open B for thirteen-to-sixteen-year-olds who, again, have won three Novice firsts.

Obedience trial competition is a very different type of show competition. As an obedience competitor, the dog is not judged on his appearance and conformation to the breed standard of perfection (although he must be purebred and registered with the AKC). Rather, he is judged on his ability to perform required activities and obey the commands of his handler. Obedience trials are often held in conjunction with all-breed or specialty shows or they can be held separately. Since obedience competition differs markedly from the conformation competitions, it has been discussed in detail in a separate chapter.

ATTAINING A CHAMPIONSHIP TITLE

While very few dogs ever attain Best In Show honors, the primary goal of most exhibitors is to have their dog reach his championship. This is generally regarded as the standard of conformation excellence. A championship title can be attained only by participation in sanctioned "point" shows—shows that award an appropriate number of championship points for placing first in the classes. The scale of points is determined by the number of dogs entered in the classes as compared to the minimum numbers of entries required by breed regulations for various pont level wins. A win of three points is called a "major." To attain a championship title, a dog must accumulate at least fifteen points under at least three judges, and there must be two major wins from different judges included in the fifteen points. It is possible to receive fifteen or more points and not qualify for championship, as the major wins are lacking. A major win generally requires the dog to be of superior quality and to defeat a large number of entries at a large show.

During the judging each dog will be judged against his breed standard of perfection. This is a set of very exacting guidelines that has been drawn up by the national breed club and approved by the American Kennel Club. It defines point by point what a perfect specimen of the breed would look, move, and act like, including such details as the desired set of the teeth, texture of the coat, shape of the head, etc. Besides pointing out the ideal, the standard also defines which characteristics are considered to be faults or disqualifications.

THE CLASSES

If your purebred is registered with the American Kennel Club, he is eligible to compete in point shows as long as he is not altered (neutered) or somehow disqualified by breed rules. Depending on his age, sex, and number of previous show wins, there are various classes in which he can be entered: Puppy, Novice, Bred-by-Exhibitor, American-bred, and Open. These five classes are defined as follows:

PUPPY CLASS: Open to dogs at least six months of age but not more than twelve months of age.

NOVICE CLASS: Open to dogs six months of age or older that have not won a first prize in any class other than Puppy Class and that have less than three first prizes in the Novice Class itself and no championship points. The class is limited to dogs whelped in the United States and Canada.

BRED-BY-EXHIBITOR CLASS: Open to all dogs, except champions, six months of age and over that are owned wholly or in part by the person or by the spouse of the person who was breeder or one of the breeders of record. The class is limited to dogs whelped in the United States or, if individually registered in The American Kennel Club Stud Book, for dogs whelped in Canada. Dogs entered in the Bred-by-Exhibitor Class must be handled by the breeder or one of the breeders of record or by a member of the immediate family of the breeder or one of the breeders of record. Members of an immediate family include husband, wife, father, mother, son, daughter, brother, or sister.

AMERICAN-BRED CLASS: Open to all dogs, except champions, six months of age or older that were whelped in the United States by reason of a mating that took place in the United States.

OPEN CLASS: Open to all dogs six months of age or older except in a member specialty club show held only for American-bred dogs, in which case the Open Class shall be only for American-bred dogs.

PREPARING FOR SHOW COMPETITION

Once you have located your show dog, or if you are lucky enough to own a puppy that is blossoming into a beautiful specimen and have received encouragement from judges at puppy matches about your dog's chances in championship competition, you must begin training yourself and your dog for the skills of the show ring. The best initial preparation is to visit a few shows and watch the goings on. Talk to the experienced exhibitors, as they are generally more than happy to extol the virtues of their breed and their particular dogs. If you plan on showing your dog yourself, study the movements of the professional handlers and their technique for controlling their dogs. Watch the judges to see what they require of the dogs and the handlers. Spending a few days mingling with the more experienced exhibitors may prove very helpful in acquiring a "feel" for the show ring.

During an actual judging, your dog will be required to gait around the show ring and be physically inspected by the judge. Before you enter any competition, train your dog to gait at a trot by your side. Teach him to hold his head high and move in a straight line. He must master this and perform it willingly to accentuate the beauty and grace of his movement, as this will be under the watchful eye of the judge.

The judge will want to closely examine the dog's physical structure. To do this, the dog will need to calmly stand for examination and allow the judge to run his hands over the dog's body. The judge will carefully feel the body contours and examine the teeth. Teach the dog to stand squarely with his head erect and the hind

243

legs positioned slightly back. It is easiest to familiarize the dog to this position if you routinely "stack" or set him in this manner every time you groom him. He should learn to stay in this stacked position for at least two minutes.

Practice gaiting and stacking the dog as if you were in competition and the dog will quickly become accustomed to the procedure. If possible, have another person simulate the role of the judge by running his hands over the dog's body during your practice sessions. This will acquaint him with the feel of a stranger's touch. It is essential that the dog learn to be at ease during such examinations, as exhibiting any signs of aggression or biting during the judging will spoil any chance of show ring success.

Handling classes can be an aid for both handler and dog. Local dog clubs usually sponsor a series of classes run by a professional handler or a very experienced exhibitor to help novice exhibitors correct any faults they may have in their showing technique. For a modest fee you can be critiqued on your strengths and weaknesses and instructed on how to highlight your dog's best features through good presentation. Handling instruction should not be confused with obedience instruction, as your dog should have mastered the basic obedience commands prior to his beginning any ring work. Instruction in handling is intended to help dog and owner become an efficiently working team—working *with*, not against each other.

ENTERING A DOG SHOW

When—and only when—you feel confident that both you and your dog have mastered the basic requirements for the ring, it is time to enter a point show. By reading the local dog club bulletins or the national dog publications you can find the location and dates of shows in your area. Write to the show superintendent or secretary listed with the show information and he or she will supply you with the official entry form and all necessary applications. A listing of the American Kennel Club sanctioned point shows can routinely be found in such magazines as *Pure-bred Dogs/American Kennel Gazette, Dog World,* and *Dog Fancy.* Similarly, details which pertain to Canadian Kennel Club shows can be found regularly in the magazine *Dogs in Canada.*

244

Be sure to fill in the entry form accurately, as any mistake on official information may nullify the application. Decide which class your dog is to compete in. Novices with young dogs should begin in the Puppy Class and gradually move up the class ladder to the Open Class as handler and dog gain ring experience. Entries are generally limited to a certain number of dogs and usually close three weeks before the date of the show, so do not wait until the last moment to send in the application.

THE DAY OF THE SHOW

Before leaving for the show, be sure to pack all items you will need that day: a dog crate, water and food dishes, bottled water (to avoid a possible adverse reaction to different drinking water), food, a show lead, a chain or leash to tie him to his crate or bench area, and grooming tools. Check to see that you have in your possession the identification ticket sent to you by the show superintendent verifying your entry and stating your dog's judging time at the show. Review this information and plan your travel and arrival time accordingly.

As the trip in the car will be exciting for the dog, do not feed him the morning of the show. You may give him a dry dog biscuit or two or a very light meal if he appears hungry. Plan on giving him his main meal of the day after his judging, as a sated dog will not show as eagerly and enthusiastically as a slightly hungry one.

Upon arrival at the show, give the dog a drink of water and follow this with a trip to the exercise pen so that he can relieve himself. It is important the dog relieve himself before he is exposed to the excitement of the judging ring to avoid a possibly embarrassing ring experience.

About one hour before his judging begin his final grooming. Be sure to give him a chance to relax before the judging. A few minutes before your class is to be called, take him to the ring and check in with the ring steward, who will then give you your arm band.

CLOTHING

It is important to dress the part of a dog show competitor. The emphasis should be on presenting a neat appearance while wearing clothes that are comfortable and allow you ease of movement.

Wang's Ts'ai Shen is gaited around the ring for examination by the judge **(top)**. Gold's Black Magic of Bedlam and her handler, Heather Wang, won first place in Junior Showmanship competition **(bottom)**. Both dogs owned by the Wangs of Lexington, Kentucky.

Shoes are especially important. Select a pair with rubber, nonslip soles and be sure they are comfortable enough to spend an active afternoon in.

Clothing should be appropriate for the occasion—neither too formal nor too informal. You should be able to gait with your dog around the ring without restriction from tight clothes. If possible, wear an outfit with a small pocket to hold small supplies or bait. Avoid clothing that is too loose and do not wear dangling jewelry, as these can be distracting to the dog while you both are in motion around the ring.

Color is also important, as you want to wear clothing that is not so dark that it easily displays hairs or dusty paw prints. Your clothing should blend, not distract, from the coloring of your dog. You do not want to appear so similar in color that you merge together with your dog. As a rule, if you own a dark- colored dog you should wear clothing that is slightly lighter than his coat. This will set a pleasing contrast between owner and dog.

One last point to remember: be prepared for all types of weather, especially if you are attending an outdoor show. Always carry rain gear. Have a sweater or light jacket handy to add or take off as the conditions change.

IN THE RING

Once you have checked in with the steward and your class is called, take your place with the other competitors. Be sure that you have placed your arm band on your left arm, at the top so it can be easily seen by the judge and the steward.

Get in line and position yourself accordingly—not too close or too far from the other entries. Listen to the instructions of the judge and proceed as he or she requests. Both handler and dog are expected to conduct themselves in a "gentlemanly" fashion in the ring, showing courtesy not only to the judge but to the other competitors as well.

GAITING

One of the key aspects in the judging process is to review the dog's gait. The judge will ask the handler to move the dog around the ring to assess the dog's grace and ease of movement. The dog should always be placed on your left side, and you retain control by holding the leash in your left hand. It is imperative that you practice this action until you are sure the dog will remain under control during the actual judging process. This is an important maneuver, as it often imparts the first impression of your dog in the judge's mind.

There are several common patterns that the judges use to evaluate a dog's gait. The most common is to move the entire class of dogs under evaluation around the ring in a circular pattern, usually reversing the pattern after a revolution or two around the ring. The dog should be gaiting freely, on as loose a lead as possible.

During the individual examination of your dog the judge may ask you to gait the dog "out and back," in a "triangle," in the "circular" pattern, or in a pattern of his choice that he feels will give him the best view of those aspects of the gait that he cares to evaluate.

When moving the dog for the judge, the point to keep in mind always is to present the dog at his best. The dog should always be kept between you and the judge so that you do not obscure the judge's view. Control is of the utmost importance because it shows the judge that you and the dog are confident and well prepared for the show ring.

JUDGING PROCEDURE

The classes for the male dogs will be called first, in this order: Puppy, Novice, Bred-by-Exhibitor, American-bred, and Open. The winner in each class is selected and then competes for the Winners Dog title. Only the Winners Dog is awarded points toward his championship title, the number of points being decided by the number of dogs participating in the breed competition. The procedure is then repeated for the female entries. This time, the class winners compete for the title of Winners Bitch. Reserve Winners Dog and Reserve Winners Bitch are also named at this point, but they do not receive any championship points.

Winners Dog and Winners Bitch then move on to compete against each other for Best of Winners. They are then placed against the Specials (champions) for the Best of Breed and Best of Opposite Sex to the Best of Breed titles. Best of Breed is the top breed award, and this winner goes on to represent the breed in the

Lori Poindexter **(top)** handles Bedlam's Mei-Mei Ling to Winners Bitch and Best of Opposite Sex for a five-point "major" at Clermont County, 1984. Breeder, Ellen Weathers Debo; owners, the Wangs of Lexington, Kentucky. Kim Lee Lotus Blossom-Tezak, a bitch owned by Pat and Jerry Brown of Pai Gai Kennels, Honey Brook, Pennsylvania, pictured going Best of Breed at the Chinese Shar-pei Club of America Northeast Specialty Show, 1985 **(bottom).**

A well-balanced Shar-pei should be able to "stack" itself, standing squarely with head erect **(top)**. Additionally, when moving the dog around the ring, you should be able to show it on a loose lead, *i.e.,* there should be no need to "string" the dog up. Early show training for a promising show puppy is essential **(bottom).**

Oriental Treasure's Sha Do at three months going Best of Breed Junior Puppy. Breeder/ owner, Maryann Smithers of Boonton, New Jersey.

Group competition. At this level all Best of Breed winners from the specific groups are judged against their own breed standards and first, second, third, and fourth place winners are selected. These dogs are chosen by the judge as the best breed representatives and the first place winner moves on to represent his group in the Best In Show competition. From these Group winners (the Groups are Sporting breeds, Hound breeds, Working breeds, Terrier breeds, Toy breeds, Non-sporting breeds and Herding breeds) the judge selects one dog as the best specimen of the day—the Best in Show.

251

A two-and-a-half-week-old puppy from Bedlam Kennels, bred by Ellen Weathers Debo. This little guy has quite a sense of humor!

Index